JOURNEY TO GOD

JOURNEY TO GOD

Anglican Essays
on the Benedictine Way

ISBN 0 906990 00 9

Set in Perpetua type and
designed, printed and bound at
St. Mary's Abbey, West Malling, Kent.

Contents

Our contributors

Aelred Arnesen is the founder and spiritual father of the Anglican cistercian community at Ewell Monastery.

Louis Weil is Professor of Liturgics at Nashotah House, Wisconsin, U.S.A. The author of numerous articles, he is also co-author of *Liturgy for Living* (Seabury Press, 1979).

Roger Greenacre is Chancellor and Canon Residentiary of Chichester Cathedral and acts as Senior Ecumenical Officer for the diocese. He was for ten years Chaplain at St. George's, Paris.

Esther de Waal is a historian. She is married to Victor de Waal, Dean of Canterbury, and has four sons.

Introduction

1980 sees the celebration of the fifteen hundredth anniversary of the birth of St. Benedict, patriarch of Western monasticism. What has this to do with Anglicans? Much in every way. To begin with the English Church owes its foundation and organisation to monks, Augustine and his companions, sent by Pope Gregory in 597 to preach the gospel to the heathen folk of this remote island. The missionaries brought with them the *vita monachica* and it was the minsters (or monasteries) which became centres of education for Latin Christianity together with its culture. Through Augustine the English Church was from the first drawn into the main stream of Western Christendom, whereas the Celtic Church, for all its missionary activity, art and learning, lay outside it. The first great English scholar, Bede, was the fruit of a process set in motion by Augustine in the short seven years of his episcopate at Canterbury.

The benedictine Rule spread slowly, gradually superseding all other monastic rules until the rise of the new orders of friars in the thirteenth century. These benedictine centuries left an enduring mark on the English Church, not only in the men who became bishops and archbishops and statesmen in the service of the king, but also in the tradition of liturgical prayer which survived the Reformation and is continued in the daily offices of our cathedrals and parish churches. The ideal of a life consecrated wholly to God persisted, despite the dissolution of the monasteries, as is evident from the writings of some of the Caroline Divines and Jeremy Taylor. It found concrete expression at Little Gidding and the household at Kingscliffe directed by William Law. Since the revival of the religious life in the Church of England in the nineteenth century, the Rule has been used by several communities as the basis of their own rule, while others have adopted it *in toto*.

There is a true affinity between benedictine and Anglican spirituality; both are rooted in Scripture, the liturgy and the writings of the Fathers. The Rule draws on a monastic tradition common to East and West and it is to the centuries before the schism between the Eastern Church and Rome that the Church of England also looks. It is noticeable that in their long history benedictines have seldom been drawn to this or that devotion or caught up in ecclesiastical fashions. With Anglicans their spirituality shares a certain sobriety and realism and above all liberty for the individual. The Rule lays down no method of prayer, but leaves the monk free for the inspiration of the Spirit.

It seems right therefore that Anglicans should contribute in some small measure to the celebrations in 1980. Three of the essays in this volume come from those who live directly under the Rule. Three come from those who do not; their contribution is for this reason all the more valuable and we are indeed grateful to them. Fr. Weil assesses the principles which lie behind the importance of the *opus Dei*; Canon Greenacre describes the work of benedictines in the cause of christian unity; Esther de Waal analyses the benedictine tradition in its application to family life. All witness to the vitality and relevance of the Rule. Benedict himself may seem a somewhat remote and shadowy figure, but his 'little Rule for beginners' is as timeless as the gospel and as incisive. At the heart of the Rule, as of the gospel, stands the Christ who calls us to choose the narrow way that leads to life and with him to journey to God.

To our benedictine brothers and sisters who are journeying Godwards in the joy of the holy Spirit, this book is dedicated with love and gratitude and the prayer that he will bring us all alike to life everlasting.

St. Mary's Abbey,
West Malling,
Kent.

Errata

Page 4 : 'fourth book of the *Dialogues*' should read 'second book'.

Page 7 : For 'Eleanor' read 'Isabella'.

Pages 19 and 26 : The year of Fr. Vasey's death should be 1931.

Malling Abbey
and the revival of the benedictine life
in the Anglican Church

The chief figure in the revival of the benedictine life in the Church of England was undoubtedly Benjamin Fearnley Carlyle, better known as Abbot Aelred Carlyle, who made his profession as a benedictine in 1898. Yet as early as 1863 the eccentric Father Ignatius —Joseph Lyne—had founded a benedictine brotherhood and he was responsible too for the establishment of the first community of benedictine sisters in 1868, with Reverend Mother Hilda Stewart as their superior. It was due to her courage and determination that the Community of SS. Mary and Scholastica survived while Father Ignatius's community for men died out. In his book *Abbot Extraordinary* Peter Anson has recounted Abbot Aelred's career in detail, his connection with Father Ignatius and Mother Hilda and his eventual secession to Rome. Here we shall sketch only the history of Malling Abbey and how our own community came to follow the Rule of St. Benedict and eventually to find our home here.

MALLING ABBEY was founded by Gundulf, bishop of Rochester, about the year 1090. Yet the little town of West Malling is much older than the Norman Gundulf. There are indications that the Romans were here, but it was not until the last decades of the fifth century, perhaps in 480, the very year of St. Benedict's birth, that a certain Meallo settled with his people near the spring and the place received the name of Meallingas. Some hundred years later Pope Gregory the Great, to whose fourth book of the *Dialogues* we owe almost everything we know about St. Benedict, sent Augustine and a band of monks to convert these pagan peoples. One of them, Justus, became the first bishop of Rochester. He built a church there, and homesick perhaps for his monastery on the Caelian Hill, dedicated it to St. Andrew. Three centuries later lands at Malling were given by the king of Kent to Burhric, the then bishop of Rochester. In the confusion of the Danish wars the Malling lands were lost to the church, but after the Norman conquest they were eventually recovered and a new era opened with the consecration of Gundulf as bishop in 1077.

Gundulf had been a monk of Bec where

4

Lanfranc had been his prior and Anselm, with whom he formed a life-long friendship, his contemporary. His first task at Rochester was the rebuilding of the Saxon church and then with Lanfranc's close co-operation the establishment of a monastic foundation modelled on that of Canterbury. The small body of four or five canons was replaced by a community of benedictine monks to whom the bishop was both an example and their instructor in the monastic life. With his cathedral rebuilt, his community established and in 1087 the body of St. Paulinus translated to a new shrine, Gundulf 'beloved by both sexes' turned his attention to the foundation of a convent of nuns.

For the site of this new foundation he chose his manor of Malling. The *Vita Gundulfi* tells us that the place 'formerly consisted of fields and had few inhabitants, but as a number of people flocked there to help in building a house for the bishop, the place is now well populated'.[1] The bishop's house was the stone keep known today as St. Leonard's Tower, the earliest surviving Norman keep in England and well situated to protect the episcopal manors in the Medway Valley. We can imagine Gundulf riding over from Rochester to the keep and then, following the course of the Ewell stream which furnished the nuns with their water supply, walking down to inspect the progress of the domestic buildings and the fine stone church in honour of the blessed virgin Mary. Before he left he would gather the community together to instruct them in the wisdom and discipline of the monastic life.

We learn from the *Vita* that the bishop procured experienced nuns from other convents—perhaps from the abbey at Caen where his own mother had ended her days—to guide his foundation at Malling. He refused to appoint an abbess, preferring to govern the community himself and only when he was dying, urged by letters from the king and Archbishop Anselm, who had bestowed his manor of East Malling on the convent, did Gundulf finally consent to nominate the prioress, Avicia, as abbess. She was summoned to his bedside in the monks' infirmary at Rochester and there 'he took a pastoral staff and with many standing round delivered it to the prioress, making her the first abbess of that house'.[2] Gundulf died on 8 March 1108.

6

So Malling Abbey was founded and for four and a half centuries continued as a benedictine house. Its history is much like that of any other medieval nunnery, its fortunes fluctuating with the accidents of fire, of pestilence and sometimes of the political scene. In 1190 a disastrous fire destroyed much of the town and convent, while the Black Death in 1349 reduced the community to four professed and four novices. In 1206 King John usurped the nuns' right to appoint their own prebendary and nominated his chancellor, John de Gray; in 1321 the abbess, Elisabeth de Badlesmere, was forced to resign when her brother Bartholomew, custodian of Leeds Castle, refused entrance to Edward II's queen, Eleanor.

The various building operations undertaken at Malling show that the community had a certain resilience and power of recovery through the centuries. Gundulf's original church, with its long aisleless nave, north and south transepts and shallow tower at the crossing, its rectangular east end and elaborate west front, underwent considerable extension in the thirteenth century. The beautiful ornamented arcade in the south cloister was already begun when King

7

John was at Malling in 1208. The Gate House, in all probability the prebendal lodging adjoining the almonry with its chapel dedicated to St. Thomas of Canterbury, was built in the fourteenth century. The same period saw the incorporation of the octagon into the west front and further alterations to the church.[3]

In the years immediately preceding the dissolution there was considerable competition among the local gentry for the office of high steward to the abbey. The abbess, Elisabeth Read, showed herself neither submissive nor compliant to Thomas Cromwell or even to the king's wishes in the matter. Clearly she would not easily surrender the abbey and in February 1537 Margaret Vernon was elected in her place. Margaret had formerly been prioress of Little Marlow and now at Malling she was to repeat the surrender of a religious house to the Crown. Although the nuns must have known for more than a year what was in store for them they would have had no inkling on 29 October 1538 that they had attended Mass and sung the office for the last time. On the morning of that day, without warning even to Margaret Vernon, Cromwell's agents, Drs. Layton and Peter,

8

arrived to demand the surrender of the abbey and all its property. There was no possibility of refusal and the nuns gave their consent. The Malling Deed[4] follows a standard pattern emphasising that the abbess and nuns, after considering the matter, of their own accord, willingly agree to concede everything to the illustrious Prince and Lord, King Henry VIII. It bears the convent seal but there are no signatures. Did the nuns make a last gesture of protest and refuse to sign the document ?

So the history of Malling Abbey as a house of benedictine nuns came to an end. It suffered the same fate as monasteries throughout England. The church was gradually demolished, only the west front, a stretch of the south nave wall and the south transept were left standing. The property passed into secular hands, never remaining long in any one family. In the mid-eighteenth century it was owned by a London banker, Fraser Honeywood, who built the present Georgian mansion. His fine new house in Gothic style brought him shortlived happiness, for his only son died at the age of nineteen and once again the property passed into other hands.

The year 1850 was to prove a turning point in the long history of the abbey. T. S. Eliot in *Little Gidding* speaks of history as a pattern of timeless moments. A young girl's chance visit to Glastonbury Abbey, where prayer had also been valid, was one such moment. Charlotte Boyd came to Glastonbury in the summer of 1850 as one of a pleasure party. Of the once magnificent church how little remained; everywhere the stonework was broken by small bushes and flowering weeds or wreathed in ivy, while the ground, rough and undulating, was covered with coarse grass which often concealed fragments of masonry. In the distance was the Tor where the last abbot, Richard Whyting, had been hanged. Charlotte, suddenly out of sympathy with her companions, detached herself from the chattering party and found a place where she could contemplate the desolate scene undisturbed. For her there was nothing romantic or picturesque in these ruins recalling merely a vanished past. The life once lived in these walls had been offered to God and she knew that attempts had already been made to revive the religious life in the Church of

10

England under the guidance of Dr. Pusey,
Dr. Neale and others. Could these stones live
again, the ruined abbeys of England be restored
to their former glory, could she give her life
for such a cause ? Moved by a sudden impulse
she knelt and offered herself for the work of
restoration if God would accept her. Then
almost afraid of what she had done she rose and
rejoined her friends who teased her for being
so melancholy.

The years passed, but the desire kindled by
this experience remained, though she did not
speak of it except to God. Then in 1865, a few
months before his death, she asked Dr. Neale's
advice and, as might have been expected from
such a lover of England's medieval past, met
only with encouragement : 'I would have you
take it as your life's work'. Ten years later
with the support of Father Benson of Cowley
she established the English Abbey Restoration
Trust whose object was the recovery of property
which had been alienated from the Church.
The means employed were to be first, constant
prayer, and secondly, the collection of funds to
be administered by three members of the Society
of St. John the Evangelist. By 1878 when Miss

Boyd wrote an account of the Trust for an early number of *Our Work*, the magazine begun that year by the Sisters of the Church, the Trust numbered about a thousand members, including thirteen religious communities, and more than four hundred priests took part in its round of a daily Eucharist.

It was not until 1892 that the opportunity for the purchase of an ancient abbey presented itself. An *Occasional Paper* issued in 1887 by the E.A.R.T. states that 'in 1883 the Gate House at Malling Abbey was placed at the disposal of the Trust through the generous kindness of its owner. It has been utilised as a small orphanage and has attached to it a beautifully restored chapel, to which the vicar of the parish is glad to welcome clergy who wish to assist at its services.'[5] The generous owner was Isabella Akers, widow of Aretas Akers who had purchased the abbey in 1850 for the sum of £3,600. He died in 1855, to be followed a year later by his eldest son, the Reverend Aretas Akers. It was in memory of her husband and son that Mrs Akers and her devout Tractarian family restored the Gate House chapel, which had been used as a carpenter's shop, and on All Saints day 1858 it was opened for divine worship.

Miss Boyd must often have been at Malling for the orphanage was an offshoot of the one at Kilburn which she founded in 1866. Old Mrs Akers died in 1891 and when a year later her grandson, Aretas Akers Douglas, decided to sell the property it was Charlotte Boyd who bought it for the sum of £11,000. Here at last was an opportunity to build up the waste places and restore an ancient abbey to its original use. Miss Boyd was by then an associate of the small Anglican benedictine Community of SS. Mary and Scholastica at Twickenham whose Reverend Mother Hilda Stewart had already exercised such a profound influence on the young medical student, Ben Carlyle, and his plans for a bene-dictine foundation for men. Contrary to her first intentions Miss Boyd did not use E. A. R. T. funds for the purchase of Malling Abbey, but instead created a second Trust making the abbey over to the Community of SS. Mary and Scholastica. She wished, however, that there should be a close link between the two Trusts for two members of S. S. J. E. were to serve on both. A clause in the Malling Trust provided that should the community be dissolved, or the

13

trustees so decide, the property should revert to the E.A.R.T. Both Trust Deeds were so worded that any property administered by the trustees was to be held strictly for the Church of England. Miss Boyd herself became a Roman Catholic about 1896, but the two Trusts remained unaltered.

Mother Hilda's community came to Malling in April 1893 and it was in their chapel, the south transept of the Norman church, that Ben Carlyle, now known as Fr. Aelred, made his profession as a benedictine monk in 1898 with Archbishop Frederick Temple's authorisation. He continued to keep in touch with the community and when Mother Hilda died on 28 December 1906 after years of blindness and failing health it was to him that the nuns turned for help. At his suggestion Sister Mary Pauline Ewart of the All Saints Sisters was elected abbess; under her leadership the community at Malling grew rapidly and in 1911 moved to St. Bride's Abbey, Milford Haven, to be nearer to Carlyle and his community on Caldey Island. The outcome is well known: in March 1913 the the monks of Caldey and the nuns of St. Bride's were received into the Roman Church. After

the secession of the Community of SS. Mary
and Scholastica the remaining trustees of Malling Abbey agreed to put into effect the clause
which allowed the property to be handed over
to the E. A. R. T.   Two law suits followed,
but by 1915 Malling Abbey was in the hands of
the trustees of the E. A. R. T. and its tenancy
was offered to our community, who moved
to Malling from Baltonsborough in December
1916.

Let us trace in more detail how our community came to have a part in the revival of the
benedictine life in the Church of England.
Founded on St. Mary Magdalene's day in 1891
by Jessie Park Moncrieff, the aim of the Community of the Holy Comforter was the conversion
of sinners and its scope that of an active
sisterhood. For some months the sisters worked
at Miss Boyd's orphanage in Kilburn, while
two were in charge of the orphans at Malling.
With the impending arrival of Mother Hilda's
community the Gate House orphanage was
closed and in December 1892 the sisters were
invited by the Reverend Edmund Ware to

15

undertake parish work at St. Mary's, Upper Edmonton. Here the community remained for the next fourteen years, growing steadily, establishing a school and dispensary, training girls for domestic service as well as undertaking the usual round of parish work.

How was it that this small but flourishing community should by 1906 have moved from Edmonton to a village in Somerset and exchanged their rule for that of St. Benedict? Among the more remote causes were the ritual controversies of the time: the decision of the two archbishops in 1899 that the use of incense was illegal and Archbishop Temple's injunction in 1900 that the Church of England did not admit of the reservation of the consecrated elements in any form. At St. Mary's, Upper Edmonton, the blessed sacrament was reserved and incense used and Fr. Ware was among the incumbents who refused to accept the episcopal ruling. In 1901 Mandell Creighton, bishop of London, died suddenly and was succeeded by the young bishop of Stepney, A. F. Winnington Ingram. Creighton had been the Community of the Holy Comforter's Visitor, but since the sisters were working in a rebel parish they would have been

16

reluctant to ask his successor to accept the office. Sometime during this period the young abbot of Painsthorpe, Aelred Carlyle, preached at St. Mary's, appealing for funds with his accustomed, almost hypnotic, charm and describing in glowing terms the revival of the contemplative benedictine life in the Church of England. The sisters would have been in the congregation and would doubtless have met him afterwards. In 1903 they asked him to become their Visitor and after his first visitation in November that year they began to move gradually in the direction of the enclosed benedictine life.

In a letter written to the abbot in 1909 Reverend Mother Monica speaks of their adoption of the benedictine life as the realisation of the Mother Foundress's life-long hopes and ambitions during thirty years of religious life. Jessie Moncrieff had originally belonged to a Scottish community founded in Edinburgh on St. Benedict's day, 21 March 1872. She herself had been professed on the same feast, taking as her second name that of Benedicta. How far she had studied the Rule it is impossible to tell, but the rule of the Community of the

Holy Comforter is said to have been curiously benedictine in character. The months spent caring for the orphans at Malling would have increased her interest and if, as seems probable, she kept in touch with Mother Hilda she would have known of Carlyle's profession and his subsequent foundation. On his side Abbot Aelred no doubt saw in this small community the nucleus of what might become a congregation, including not only houses of monks, but also of nuns, and his compelling enthusiasm and drive would have done the rest.

The sisters were pledged to parish work but significant changes were made in preparation for the time when they would be able to adopt the benedictine rule. In March 1904 they began to use the Latin breviary—no English translation of the benedictine office was then available—and to rise for the night office. In 1905 the way opened for them to leave Edmonton. The grant from the London Church Fund was withdrawn because of Fr. Ware's refusal to comply with the bishop's ruling on reservation and the use of incense, and the parish could no longer support the sisters. They were now free to begin their life as benedictines in earnest.

A suitable house belonging to the church was found in the village of Baltonsborough, the reputed birthplace of St. Dunstan, one of England's greatest benedictine sons, and within reasonable distance of Caldey to which Abbot Aelred and his community were to return in October 1906. Extra buildings of galvanised iron were added, including the chapel, and in the early summer of 1906 the move from Edmonton was accomplished.

Abbot Aelred came for his visitation in September and on 12 September, the feast of St. Eanswythe, the professed sisters took their simple benedictine vows. Carlyle remained their Visitor until 1913 but two factors were to limit his influence on the community. The first was the appointment of the Reverend F. P. Vasey as their chaplain in March 1907, a position he retained until his sudden death on 9 April 1932. The son of a mixed marriage—his mother was a Roman Catholic—he had been brought up in his father's faith, while his sisters followed their mother's. Such an arrangement could have resulted in divided loyalties, but in Fr. Vasey it inspired a deep longing for christian unity and also gave him a wide practical knowledge of the Roman Church. He belonged to the advanced Anglo-Catholic party, but he had a strong sense of loyalty and obedience to the Church of England and its bishops, while his obvious sincerity would often disarm prejudices and win the trust of those whose churchmanship differed radically from his own. He was only thirty-nine when he came to Baltonsborough and it must have been a lonely, uneventful and somewhat narrow sphere of life for a priest, but he saw the direction of the community as a vocation from God and it was he, rather than the abbot, who laid the foundation of the community's benedictine life, giving instructions on the Rule, prayer, the divine office and plainchant.

The second factor was the election of Sister Mary Pauline Ewart as abbess by the Community of SS. Mary and Scholastica in February 1907. Abbess Scholastica, as she became, was an extremely able woman with an excellent business head as well as a strong, forceful character. She was considerably older than the abbot and in her he found one who could sympathise with his continually expanding schemes and give them far more support than the Baltonsborough community. There could hardly be a greater contrast in his eyes between the small house and ugly iron buildings which our community occupied in an out of the way Somerset village and Malling Abbey with all the mystique of a pre-dissolution benedictine foundation. Nor was there any sister at Baltonsborough as outstanding as Abbess Scholastica, so it is scarcely surprising that almost at once the 'premier position' in the congregation was accorded to the Malling community. Given, too, the difference in Fr. Vasey's conception of the contemplative life as essentially a hidden one with no courting of publicity, and his desire to lay solid foundations rather than achieve quick outward results, it was inevitable that difficulties would ensue. By 1911 the abbot was writing to suggest that the Baltonsborough community might 'care to sever the very slight connection that exists between us'. In the event he remained their Visitor, but when the Caldey and St. Bride's communities were received into the Roman Church the nuns at Baltonsborough were unaffected by the decision in that they had no wish to follow their example.

Unaffected they could not be in that

21

everything benedictine was now suspect. A tiny remnant of the Caldey community was established at Pershore, but in August 1915 Dom Anselm Marden, the one monk in solemn vows, returned to Caldey and was received into the Roman Church. This only increased the difficulties and Brother Denys Prideaux, an oblate who had been guest master at Caldey and who was undoubtedly the most erudite of the community, was now left to carry on at Pershore. Br. Denys was not yet professed and Fr. Vasey appealed to the bishop of Bath and Wells for permission to officiate himself at clothings and professions at Baltonsborough, but this was refused.

Disappointment over the secession of Caldey and St. Bride's seems to have spurred a number of leading Anglo-Catholics to an even greater determination that the benedictine life should continue in the Church of England. Letters of sympathy and encouragement reached Baltonsborough from Lord Halifax, the Duke of Argyll, who hoped that 'in the fulness of time the community's destiny may be to send out many an offshoot to repeople and replenish the the ruined Abbeys of this land',[6] and from many priests. Fr. Howell of St. Mary's, Graham Street expressed the somewhat quaintly worded opinion that 'it is essential that the flag of the contemplative life should be kept at the top of the mast in the Church of England'.[7] The Duke of Argyll was already suggesting in a letter to Athelstan Riley that the Baltonsborough nuns should move to Malling and 'in this way what is one of the poorest, devoutest, yet least realized of communities might gather a few more friends and helpers around it'.[8]

With the bishop's refusal to authorise clothings or professions as well as the fact that the buildings at Baltonsborough were now too small, it was vital that the community should find a new home. Yet more than three years were to elapse before the Duke's suggestion became an accomplished fact. As we have seen it was not until 1915 that Malling Abbey finally came into the possession of the E. A. R. T. and the trustees, of whom Fr. W. B. O'Brien acted as secretary, were faced with the task of finding a tenant. Formal application for the Baltonsborough community was made through friends, and in July 1915 Fr. O'Brien was writing to Fr. Vasey welcoming the idea and giving details of

23

the terms of the Trust. Letters to Bishop Harmer of Rochester followed, as Fr. Vasey was insistent that the community must have his permission to settle in the diocese. To a second and third letter there was disconcertingly no reply and by January 1916 Fr. O'Brien was writing to know if the community wished to proceed with their application and asking for a definite reply by the trustees' next meeting in February. Convinced that action must be taken and the episcopal stronghold stormed Fr. Vasey appealed for help to Fr. H. F. B. Mackay of All Saints, Margaret Street. He undertook to approach Canon Dawson, Rector of Chislehurst. In the next fortnight letters, reaching Baltonsborough from London the next day and all for the sum of one penny, and telegrams went to and fro. Eventually an interview was arranged between the bishop and Fr. Vasey at Canon Dawson's house. The outcome was entirely satisfactory: Fr. Vasey was given permission to officiate in the diocese and authorised to take professions and clothings. The way was open for the move from Baltonsborough to Malling.

The abbey had been empty for more than

five years and much had to be done in the way of repairs and alterations. An appeal, signed by Lord Halifax, was launched for the sum of not less than £2,500 and a copy circulated in the *Cowley Evangelist*. The last paragraph of the appeal speaks of 'the special opportunities of the Benedictine Order for promoting that re-union of Christendom for which we all so earnestly pray and the need of which was never more urgent than it is at this time'. These words seemed to the community to lay on them a special obligation to deepen and intensify their prayer for christian unity.

It was not until December 1916 that the abbey was ready for re-occupation and the move accomplished, not only with the difficulties attendant in war time, but at a moment when most of the community were recovering from influenza. The first years at Malling were ones of hardship and real poverty, but it was now possible for clothings and professions to take place and for the noviceship to develop under Sister Maud Mary, who later was our first Reverend Mother to take the title of abbess. It was a time of consolidation and growth; in 1929 the building of the guest chapel completed our

enclosure and in July of that year the professed
sisters took their solemn vows. After Fr. Vasey's
death in 1932 Fr. O'Brien S.S.J.E. became
the community's spiritual director and for
twenty-five years was to enrich us with his
wisdom and spiritual insight. In these years
there was little to distinguish us outwardly from
Roman Catholic benedictine communities with
whom we had in common the Latin Mass and
office, Declarations on the Rule, grilles and
strict enclosure. The quality of hiddenness
which Fr. Vasey considered an essential of the
contemplative life remained as part of his
spiritual legacy to the community. It was this
perhaps that gave us the tacit acceptance and
even the friendship of Bishop Harmer and of
successive bishops of Rochester, however little
they might approve of all we did and especially
of our Latin office.

The years following Vatican II have brought
many changes for us as for all religious communities, whether Roman or Anglican. The
foundations of our benedictine life had been laid
in the only way possible, that of conformity
to the existing model of Catholic benedictine
nuns. More than once before the renewal

26 .

which has allowed of experiment and pluralism we had been urged to use our freedom, and yet if our house had not been firmly grounded in the benedictine tradition it might have collapsed before the strong wind of change. Already in the fifties we were returning to the sources: of the Rule in Cassian and St. Basil and the desert fathers; of worship through the study of the early liturgies; of the Bible through Fr. Lionel Thornton C.R. who for many years was our instructor in the scriptures. He taught us, quoting St. Augustine, how 'in the new the old lies open, and in the old the new lies hid'; and above all the meaning of *koinonia*, our common life in the Body of Christ. More recently we have turned to the sources of our Anglican heritage, the writings of the Caroline divines, permeated as they are with those orthodox Catholic Fathers whom St. Benedict wished his monks to study. It was during these years that an Orthodox nun shared our life and we came to know the riches of the Orthodox liturgy and spirituality. Gradually we abandoned Latin and now after a period of experiment we have our own English office and liturgy. Grilles have dis-appeared and our enclosure has been extended so that we can be entirely responsible for the Guest House, and for our big kitchen garden and orchards—but we are not anxious to go further afield.

All these changes, together with the warm support and friendship of our diocesan, Bishop David Say, have resulted in our complete integration into the diocese. It is worth recording, perhaps, that Bishop Harmer in his letter to Canon Dawson, arranging for his interview with Fr. Vasey, reflected the current suspicion of everything benedictine, in saying that he could not become Visitor or patron, bless the house or invest sisters or novices. Those days are past; Bishop Say blessed our new cloister and comes regularly for professions. In 1966 he consecrated the new abbey church when our Visitor, the archbishop of Canterbury, Dr. Michael Ramsey, preached. We are glad to welcome the Dean and Chapter of Rochester and an increasing number of priests from the diocese for conferences and retreats. In 1973 advantage was taken of a clause in the Trust Deed and the property was transferred from the E.A.R.T. to the diocese to be held in trust for the Church of England. The wheel has come full circle and Malling Abbey has returned to Rochester.

A great source of joy has been the happy and fruitful contacts with Roman Catholic benedictine communities in England and abroad, ranging from Poland to Nigeria. We have found that to live under the same rule produces a family likeness and characteristics that transcend our different ecclesiastical allegiance; we are all one in Christ. With the community at Bec we have a specially close link of which the ceramic of St. Anselm and Gundulf given by the abbot and monks on the occasion of the consecration of our new church is a constant reminder.

What of the future ? We live in times of great uncertainty when for many the christian faith is no longer credible and the Church irrelevant. Will the benedictine life survive to celebrate another centenary ? Other essays in this book speak of the values enshrined in the Rule and the way of life it engenders. Men are still hungry for these values for our brave new world has betrayed us. If those who come after can hold fast to the principles of this very little Rule for beginners there will still be monks and nuns to give thanks for the birth of our holy Father Benedict in the year 2080. May we venture a less distant hope. A benedictine monk, Basil Hume, is now Cardinal Archbishop of Westminster. Could the day come when the see of Canterbury is held by one shaped by the Rule as were Augustine, Dunstan, Lanfranc and Anselm; above all may the day come when Rome and Canterbury will be once more in full communion.

St. Mary's Abbey,
West Malling,
Kent.

Notes

[1] *Life of Gundulf* (ET Malling Abbey 1968) p. 57.
[2] ibid. p. 66.
[3] From notes of a lecture given to the community by Martin Biddle after his excavations 1961-62.
[4] Public Record Office, Document E322-147.
[5] E.A.R.T. papers, S.S.J.E., Oxford.
[6] From the community archives.
[7] ibid.
[8] Lambeth Palace Library, MS. 2351, ff. 139-40.

The Place

There is a place, a vantage point on rising ground at the far end of the boundary wall, from which one can look down over the monastery of St. Mary at Malling and so across nine centuries of English history. From here the ground slopes gently down towards orchard and kitchen garden with their beehives and apple trees and orderly rows of onions and cabbages. This is a fruitful land, tilled over and over, year in, year out, providing a living for past generations as it does today. Beyond the kitchen garden wall and the line of willows marking the course of the stream stands the monastery. It is a medley of diverse styles, Kentish red tiles mingling with Kentish grey-white ragstone, drawn into unity by a common purpose. Surrounding it are leisurely trees, suggestive of an English country estate and these are matched by the gracious dignity of Fraser Honeywood's eighteenth century house. Built of stones from the pillaged abbey church, it has now been reclaimed and restored to monastic use. The great tower which dominates the scene takes us further back into time, for its stones give evidence of each successive stage of the first community, from its foundation through the years of growth to the final dissolution. The high-pitched roof of the Norman nave has long ago disappeared. In its place the modern church bears witness to the vitality of the benedictine tradition which, driven underground for four centuries, has now risen, transfigured, into a new and very different age.

Benedict's vow of stability, aimed at curbing individualism among monks (for simplicity's sake the word 'monk' is taken throughout to include nuns following this same Rule of St. Benedict) has led to a certain individuality in monasteries. The early monks settled on the land they were given and put down roots. They took colour from their surroundings, they were shaped by the peculiar confluence of hill and stream, of wood and weather, as well as by the mutual interaction of their own minds and characters. Every benedictine abbey has its own autonomy and identity, though with a family likeness to all others sharing this tradition and rule. Our inheritance here at Malling is twofold. We have a vivid sense of continuity with the first community—with our medieval sisters we look to Gundulf as our founder—and we live in the place where this benedictine tradition re-entered the Anglican Church. The christian faith was brought to our land by monks and their heritage has remained inherent in the Church of England through a vernacular choir office rooted in Scripture and psalmody, which has shaped the spirituality of generations of Anglicans. The recovery of this tradition in its fulness is a return to the source and a powerful move towards healing the breach of separation between Canterbury and Rome.

The Place of Encounter

Human beings have an urge to be useful and to discover usefulness in things and people: the question 'What is it for?' is part of the search for authenticity and meaning. Monks, though, need to be a little wary of this question; on the human level it defies answering. For the secular historian monastic art, learning and agriculture are part of the on-going spread of civilisation, but looked at from within the monastery these are by-products. The Church, while recognising the monastic witness to God's paramount claim on human life, has nevertheless felt a need to credit monks with a certain human usefulness, considering them as entrusted with the recitation of the Divine Office on behalf of others, or having a special responsibility for intercession or spiritual counselling. Benedict's answer is simpler but paradoxical. The monk, he says, is to seek God, but in so doing he is the workman sought by the Lord: he is to do the work of God, yet it is God who works in him and he is to find his way to heaven through obedience and humility whose symbol is the ladder he ascends by climbing down. Benedict says nothing of any specific or direct responsibility towards those who live beyond the monastery, though he has a good deal to say about those who knock on its gates. For the monk the work of God is primary, nothing is to be put before it; his life is to be wholly God-centered and God-directed; paradox is resolved in praise.

On the face of it this suggests that Benedict had no use for the world, God's ordinary everyday world beyond the monastery. But again we have to be on our guard. We ask different questions from those of fifteen hundred years ago and the formulation of meaning so essential to us is not necessarily part of Benedict's way of thinking. We can, however, find hints and clues to help us both in the text of his Rule and still more from the experience of living it. Benedict begins with what might be termed an address to the newly-arrived postulant, couched in very direct terms to the individual who seeks to respond to God's call, warning him of the demands of the life and giving him a foretaste of the trials and joys ahead. But once past the Prologue he rarely considers the individual apart from the community and this culminates in a description in Chapter 72 of the perfecting of human relationships — charity at white heat. It is significant that the other types of monks whose way of life he describes in Chapter 1 only to leave aside, even the heroic race of anchorites, are all essentially individual. Benedict is concerned with community and moreover with a single community in a specific place. Monks are to stay in that place and not wander about outside and, as far as possible, everything they need is to be found there. It has often been pointed out that in an age when a top-heavy centralised bureaucracy was disintegrating,

37

leaving the land a prey to violence and rapacity, a measure of economic self-sufficiency was the only mode of survival. But Benedict is less concerned with economic necessity than with spiritual freedom. He is following the desert tradition that the monk should 'stay in his cell'.

For the desert fathers the cell was the place of work and the place of prayer—they plaited both together into their mats and baskets. To 'stay in one's cell' means a persevering detachment from outside activity. The solitude and the silence of the cell enable the monk to wait, to watch and to listen, to concentrate his energies and to be available for whatever God may ask. The cell is no fortress; rather it is the still centre where all dynamisms are held in equipoise. The monk who remains stilled at this centre is thereby acknowledging that initiative lies with God. In obedience he gives up his desire for self-determination in order to co-operate with the action of the holy Spirit transforming him into the likeness of Christ. In the monastery, as in the desert, each monk is to do this in the cell of his own heart. But for Benedict the whole monastery is, as it were, a cell, the cloister where all good works are to be done and the work of transformation accomplished with and through the brethren and by means of the common life. Benedict's model here is the early Church where all things were held in common. He plots the straight course whereby the novice is to travel from isolation into community, in other words he is concerned with the building up of the Body of Christ.

How do we, benedictine nuns living in the last quarter of the twentieth century, relate to this programme? If we begin with the material level, clearly the self-sufficiency Benedict advocates is neither possible nor desirable in our technological age. We share in the mutual interdependence of our one world however much we may express the traditional monastic critique of its injustices and imbalances. Nevertheless we do experience a relative degree of independence. We have to buy our flour but we can bake our bread; we can make our own habits, though from fabric that is no longer home-spun or hand-woven. We practise a range of crafts which help us to be self-supporting and provide an interlocking pattern of shared work which builds community, and meets Benedict's requirement for hard manual labour as the counterpart and companion of prayer. In this way the monastery is still a close-knit community of total sharing, a world within a world, in contrast to the fragmentation of the world beyond our doors.

Our sharing, however, does not end with material things. We bring the whole of ourselves into the monastery—our gifts and our talents, our shortcomings and our failings. All the strange polarities of our age: the violence and the compassion, the self-assertive domination of the dictators and the often no less self-assertive withdrawal of the drop-outs, all are there potentially in each one of us, and their resolution has to be achieved in this small compass, this 'cell' which provides no escape routes from ourselves, from each other, or from God. The monastery comes to be experienced as the microcosm both of the Church and the world, the place where the wider world is reflected so that it is wholly present though in miniature. The total Christ is present in each fragment of the loaf, and wherever his healing, reconciling, up-building work is done it cannot but be fruitful for the entire Body. All lives touch at their roots.

Here is the monk's place of encounter with his fellow-men. His obligation to them is immense but it is indirect for he serves them most truly in his detachment from them. The stylised medieval picture of society as made up of the man who fights, the man who works and the man who prays implied a recognition of the place of spiritual values in the life of the nation as a whole and enabled the monk to pay his debts by the free offering of his prayers. The rise of economic man has upset the balance and obscured the need, yet the monk still holds himself bound to the obligation and this is equally true of those benedictines who are called to undertake pastoral work or other forms of active apostolate. The thrust of their life is the same, their service lies in the faithful living out of life in community to which their active work is subsidiary. Here the monk is to some extent travelling blind. In acknowledging God's initiative in his life, he tacitly accepts his own ignorance of how he may be used; he is not to concern himself with the fruits. He has to attend to the Word who says 'What I am doing you do not know now, afterwards you will understand'.

There is however a more immediate place of contact: the monk answers those who knock on his gate. For Benedict, care for the guests of the monastery seems a symbol of the monk's openness to God's initiative even more than an expression of lovingkindness. Twice he says in Chapter 53 that guests are to be received as Christ, indeed that in them Christ is to be worshipped. The full force of this is obscured in our English translations, for the words: 'receive, welcome, greet' are renderings of the one word: *suscipere*. Listening to the repeated reading of the Rule, the monk would respond immediately to this word, for it would take him back to that moment in his profession when, having spoken his vows, he set the seal on his self-offering with the verse: *Suscipe me, Domine*. 'Uphold me, O Lord, that I may live.' The implication is clear: 'Welcome one another as Christ has welcomed you'. Welcomed, guest and monk together say: 'We have received your mercy, O Lord'. *Suscepimus*. Hospitality to guests is an integral part of every benedictine house, and today this must be taken to include those who write to us, together with news of people, ideas and events that claims our concern.

They come bringing the whole gamut of the world's experience and needs. They come to receive and to give; through our mutual giving and receiving we are enriched.

The Place of Prayer

Today our table fellowship with our guests is at the Eucharist, in the great circle which, together, we make round the altar. Benedict's references to the Eucharist are brief and incidental, but significantly centered on the moments of offering and communion, oscillating between the individual and corporate dimension of the monk's life. With his own hand the newly-professed monk places the chart of his vows, that is the offering of himself, on the altar. In its rightful order the community gives the kiss of peace and receives communion. We receive, we give, we are built into the Body of Christ. This, in its widest sense, is the work of God, the place of our becoming, where we are to realise and grow into that unity which already exists.

When Benedict treats of prayer the same fruitful tension is apparent. The choir office, which for him is the focal point of the work of God, is the monk's corporate offering, the service to which he has committed himself and which makes its claim upon him even out of choir, whereas the monk's own prayer is individual, spontaneous and wholly uncircumscribed. Linking the two is the slow pondering on the Word of God, whether found in Scripture or elsewhere, which is the hard work of spiritual reading—Benedict equates it with manual labour. Prayer is the natural climate of the monastery and the monk moves towards that state in which prayer flows out from the chant in choir to be the mainspring of his work and the mediator in all his dealings with his brethren.

This is not to be done in a day. Benedict has a great deal more to say about prayer than at first sight appears; he is himself so steeped in prayer that there are few words in the Rule that do not presuppose prayer in some sense as their ground. He has two main principles. The first is a total attentiveness; in choir, in singing the psalms, voice and mind are to be in harmony. Now anyone whose conscience is burdened, whose heart is harbouring a grudge or whose mind is planning the pursuits of the day ahead, is incapable of such concentration. He is divided, split, and this is our common condition. Before he attempts to pray he needs to be cleansed and healed, made a unity in himself. Benedict, again following Cassian and the desert fathers, gives guidance about preparation for prayer rather than prayer itself. Chapter 4 on the tools of good works might be termed a catalogue of hindrances to prayer. In it the monk is counselled to look into his own heart and to see how its unseen, often unconscious stirrings are vitiating his whole being and so erecting barriers cutting him off from himself, his brethren and from God.

The questioning steel of these tools is very searching. Which of us, for example, can honestly say that we give God the glory for any good we may find in ourselves without taking credit for it? Which of us has not been a subtle detractor of his brother by the weighted word, the meaningful glance? This state of dividedness requires a change of heart, a conversion. The benedictine vow of conversion of life has a technical meaning, embracing poverty and chastity. Yet it is basically the promise we share with our oblates and indeed with all our

fellow christians, to live out our baptismal vows
by a total dispossession of self and givenness in
love to our neighbour. It means the death of
our false ego so that our true self may come to
life and grow in grace. As this happens we become able to pray, for the real tool that the
monk is to return to the hand of God is his own
heart, now cleansed and made whole and so
totally at the disposal of his master.

Benedict's second principle is reverence for
God and this has a three-fold aspect. Primarily
the monk recognises the transcendent otherness
of God before whom he stands, thereby acknowledging his own nothingness. The first step
on the ladder of humility which leads him up to
God by descending from himself is this continual
awareness of God; wherever he is, whatever he
is doing, he is to know himself in God's presence. Openness to God requires openness to
others, both through admitting his faults and
putting himself at the disposal of others. He
has to reverence the image of God in the heart
of his brother. At this point we encounter the
most profound ambiguity of christian living, the
place of great joy and great suffering. Benedict
recognises both. The monk is to see Christ in

46.

his abbot and the elders who, in their wisdom, reveal him to himself and lead him in the way. He is to reverence Christ in his brethren who are lovingly to help, console and encourage him, from whom he receives so much of joy: the simple courtesy, the quick apology, the ready forgiveness, the mutual unspoken understanding, and who pray for him as he for them. He is also to love Christ in those same brethren as he patiently bears the burden of their infirmities whether bodily or of character, as they do his. Benedict in no way minimises the cost of patience; it is the cross. But to share Christ's sufferings is to enter his kingdom, to be incorporated into his Body. Here is the heart of the matter, the core of our vocation. The monk is 'to prefer nothing to Christ'. In every encounter it is Christ who calls, Christ who knocks, Christ to whom we open, Christ whom we receive, Christ into whom we are being transformed.

Reverence for God in his otherness and of his image in man brings a growing awareness of his presence in his creation, and a reverence and care for material things. The norm here is the dictum that the cellarer is to treat all the

47

goods of the monastery as the consecrated vessels of the altar. There is an earthiness in the Rule, a down-to-earthness which echoes the gospel. Everything is capable of revealing God, the whole material universe is preparing for its final consummation into a spiritual body. This concept of the spiritualising of matter brings an understanding of how the monastery can act as a magnet to those outside; reflecting the prayer and the life lived within its walls, it becomes a sacrament of the indwelling presence of God. Here is a place, a minute fraction of the earth's surface on which, at least in intention, everything is directed to God's glory. This is the other mode of the monk's indirect service to the world around him: to witness to this life into which God has called him so that it may be seen as an earnest, a foretaste of the ingathering of all things into God, that he may be all in all.

The Place of the Abbot

As we live in this tradition we come very close to the founder of it, Benedict, whose life, as Gregory the Great points out, is revealed through his words, and we approach him with a growing love and awe. Here was a man who stood before God consciously and willingly bearing the shortcomings of his disciples and, by that total identification with the 'sinless, sin-bearing and suffering servant', gained the moral authority to commend the same stance to his brethren. 'If you are treated unjustly', he says, 'take it, with patience and joy. If the load is too great, then say so, quietly and dispassionately, but if your plea is not heard, shoulder the burden: God will help you. If the going is hard, stick it out, don't run away.' He knew men through and through, being able both to discern their hidden weaknesses and to call out their latent strength. He feared neither criticism nor change, for he could perceive the will of God both in the visiting monk who might see something wrong, and in the junior brother, the one most likely to come up with new ideas. He lived in a harsh and violent age and clearly had some harsh and violent characters to deal with, but it is his compassion with the weak, the faint-hearted, the easily discouraged which reveals his greatness. His monks were his 'sons', his 'dearest brethren'; to him

49

obedience was a loving identification of will between master and disciple, while authority was Christ-like service to all.

There is a short seemingly insignificant chapter in the Rule which so illustrates Benedict's concept of the role of the abbot and the relationship between abbot and monk that it is worth examining in some detail. It is Chapter 40, which lays down the daily allowance of wine. Embedded in this chapter is a sentence which gives evidence of what we today would call a Chapter discussion, for it follows step by step all that Benedict has to say in Chapter 3 on decision making in the monastery, where he insists that the abbot shall never act independently of his monks, without seeking their advice, even in the most mundane matters. The sentence runs: 'We do, indeed, read that wine is no drink for monks; but since nowadays monks cannot be persuaded of this, let us at least agree upon this, to drink temperately and not to satiety: for wine maketh even the wise to fall away' (RB).

When we move behind these words we can reconstruct the scene, and all but overhear the very words spoken at Monte Cassino nearly fifteen hundred years ago; it is a moment when time drops away. 'Let the abbot', says Benedict in Chapter 3, 'call together the whole community and himself set forth the matter'(RB), and the monks are then to give their advice. On this occasion Benedict opens with a typical appeal to tradition. He is clearly in favour of abstinence, but his monks are divided and feelings run high. The abbot listens. He listens to what God is saying to him in his own heart and through the words of his monks; he attends to the Word that underlies the words. His charisma is to decide, to discern the will of God and mediate it to his flock, to be the place where the monk's obedience to God comes to be realised in a concrete situation. Benedict's decision is given earlier in the chapter: 'Keeping in view the needs of weaker brethren, we believe that a hemina of wine a day is sufficient for each' (RB), but we have a hint, also, of the homily which accompanied it. Benedict cared nothing for status, he could let himself be overruled; he cared very much for harmony and reconciliation, that his monks should agree among themselves. It is the burden of the common life: 'Let us agree . . . '.

The rest of this chapter reads like a gloss on this decision, as if Benedict were thinking aloud, working out its implications, and the principles he enunciates hold good throughout the Rule. Neither human beings nor things conform to a preconceived pattern. Quoting St. Paul on the distribution of gifts, Benedict recognises human diversity as God-given so that the abbot legislates for the common good 'with some misgivings', while treating each monk as a unique individual responsible in the last instance to God alone, cherishing the weak, challenging the strong. No rule therefore can meet every need and Benedict makes no attempt at a comprehensive code but gives the abbot a sovereign freedom. 'Should circumstances require more, let the superior be free to grant it.' Benedict knew how to delegate responsibility, it is part of the value he placed on the individual. He sees the abbot as interpreter and guardian of the Rule, never its slave, but, like his monks, responsible to God for all his judgments. Here he is thinking of times and places other than his own. It is this discretion and wisdom which have helped to give the Rule its flexibility and to enable benedictine monasticism to survive through fifteen centuries and spread out from its Western European milieu into very different cultures and environments.

The End and the Beginning

Benedict describes his Rule as 'little' and 'for beginners' and this has puzzled many for whom it has seemed to incorporate great demands for those far advanced. As a consequence 'this little Rule for beginners' has sometimes been taken as a self-deprecatory literary convention. It is no such thing. It is a sober statement of fact, but to appreciate Benedict's meaning we have to look at it the other way on, to begin as it were at the end. Benedict was preoccupied with a moment, a point in time or out of time, or at their point of intersection. We might call it 'the hour of our death', or 'the place of our resurrection', or more accurately the passage from the one to the other, the pasch. Whenever it is encountered it requires an act of choice and Benedict has all the gospel's urgency in the face of this choice. 'Let us rise up', he says, 'let us hasten, let us run lest we be

D

overtaken by darkness; we have only this life to profit us for eternity, the time is short'.

This moment is not however a once-for-all happening, it recurs. It is the death we encounter in every moment of living, though the awareness of our passing through is not always present to us. For most of us, beginners as we are, it happens only in flashes of illumination when we are taken out of ourselves or return to ourselves, when the familiar act or well-worn truth suddenly blazes into a new incandescence. Yet tradition speaks of those who, even in this life, have wholly passed over: the desert monk, for instance, who held up his fingers against the sky to show his painstakingly conscientious brother how he might become a total flame, or those monks in whom prayer ceases to be any sort of effort of will or conscious attentiveness but in whom it begins to flow of its own accord, like the waters of a spring.

There are many ways of expressing this moment of death and resurrection which St. Benedict himself experienced as a vision of the whole world caught in a single ray of light. St. John says very simply, 'We have passed from death to life because we love the brethren', and St. Paul, 'I live, yet not I, Christ lives in me'. It is to this moment that St. Benedict would lead his monks, the moment when they are wholly taken up into Christ. He explains in Chapter 7 how at the top of the ladder of humility a monk will pass from law to love: 'whereby he will begin to observe without labour, as though naturally and by habit, all those precepts which formerly he did not observe without fear; no longer for fear of hell, but for love of Christ and through good habit and delight in virtue' (RB). The monk's life, he says, is Lenten, which is to say it is forward looking, and he provides Lenten fare for the narrow way which leads the monk to this feast of Easter, the goal of his pilgrimage, the place where we truly begin.

We can stand where we see our monastery spread out before our eyes and this is one way of looking at it. To come down from this vantage point is like walking into the canvas of a picture come alive, moving from without to within. The stream tumbles over its miniature fall, the house rises above us, its weathered

stones warm and welcoming. When we pene-
trate its facade we come through to another
place of vision, the open space of the cloister
which illuminates the monastery from within.
Here the centuries jostle; Gundulf's tower is
buttressed by the newly completed cloister
range, while the arch through which Abbess
Avicia and her sisters daily passed into choir is
still the way which leads into the light-ringed,
free-flowing space of our church. Here the
silence is palpable; sounds enter, rise and fall,
fade away and dissolve and the silence abides,
flowing under the arcading, out from the stones.
Pantiles enclose green serenity, open to the
heavens, closed to the trivia but not to the
tensions of our God-denying yet God-desiring
world. At the heart the stream rises in its
little fountain, a spring of living water welling
up into the silence, into the place where 'our
life is hid with Christ in God'.

St. Mary's Abbey,
West Malling,
Kent.

Note

Direct quotations from the Rule (RB) are taken
from the translation of Abbot Justin McCann.

56

The Cistercian
Interpretation of the Rule

The beginnings of the cistercian way of life coincided with a remarkable period of development and expansion in Europe. 'All over northern Europe we find new villages where previously there had been waste-land . . . Colonisation began on all the frontiers of western Europe, and with colonisation there began the familiar process of military aggression. For the first time in its history western Europe became an area of surplus population and surplus productivity, and it developed all the assertive and aggressive tendencies of a rapidly developing and self-confident community.'[1] Undoubtedly the white monks found the period between the foundation of the New Monastery at Cîteaux in 1098 and St. Bernard's death in 1153 a providential time in which to attract vocations to their single-minded life of prayer and work in the solitude of the monastery. During this period Clairvaux alone established sixty-five daughter houses. From France the swiftly expanding family of cistercians established themselves in Italy, Germany, Switzerland, Austria and, above all, England. Rievaulx, founded from Clairvaux in 1132, was already making a foundation of its own at Melrose in Scotland four years later. Eight centuries later the contrast could not be greater. Western Europe is in recession and although the christian commitment is strong it is a minute fraction of the growing population and there is little understanding in the Church of the Rule of St. Benedict as one of the main practical guides for living out the gospel. And yet, in another more important way, the twelfth and late twentieth centuries are very similar. In both these periods there was and is the feeling of the need for spiritual renewal. The founders of Cîteaux wished to renew their monastic vocation as lived under the Rule of St. Benedict. That this experiment was blessed with great success and made a notable contribution to the spiritual life of the Church, not only in the first two centuries of its existence but also in the more recent revival in the past hundred years, is a secondary thing. Leaving aside then the picture that most of us have of cistercian monks belonging to an outmoded culture, whether of the Middle Ages or the Gothic revival, unforgettably enshrined in the ruins of Rievaulx, Fountains or

60

Tintern, let us turn to the inner spirit of the founders of Cîteaux.

The Rule of St. Benedict

The founding community drew up a document which formulated their aims. It is called *The Institutes* and is incorporated in the document called *The Little Exordium* which is attributed to the year 1119 but which scholars now consider to come from a later period of legislation. In the *Institutes* it is stated that the abbot and brethren of the New Monastery wished to reject what was contrary to the purity of the Rule. 'Making thus the rectitude of the Rule the foremost concern of their life, they followed or conformed to the pathway of the Rule in ecclesiastical as well as other observances. In this way, having put off the old man, they rejoiced in putting on the new.'[2] Although the practical application of this principle of observing the purity of the Rule meant for the founders a rejection of what they considered superfluities in dress, food and ornamentation, there is nowhere expressed the intention to observe the Rule to the letter. In a description of the first growth of the New

61

Monastery with the coming of Bernard and his companions, a later chapter of the *Little Exordium* tells us that 'They started to flock together there in order to place their proud necks under the sweet yoke of Christ, to love fervently the rigorous and burdensome precepts of the Rule'.[3] To follow the Rule in its purity was to encounter the experience of being inwardly renewed. St. Bernard expresses this in a famous letter. Writing to the community of St. John in the Alps in the diocese of Geneva, when their abbot had just been elected to a bishopric, he says: 'We who have chosen to lie forgotten in the house of God, so that we might no more dwell in the abode of sinners, must keep our place. Our place is abjection, is humility, is voluntary poverty, peace, joy in the Holy Spirit. Our place is under a master, under an abbot, under a rule, under discipline. Our place is to cultivate silence, to exert ourselves in fasts, vigils, prayers, manual work; and above all to keep that most excellent way which is the way of charity; and furthermore to advance day by day in these things, and to persevere in them until the last day.'[4] This—in the typical, pungent phrasing of St. Bernard, who uses the words of Scripture and the Rule to express himself—is a spiritual programme brilliantly summarising the whole scope of the Rule. The monk's pilgrimage aims at that total freedom in Christ by voluntarily submitting to the Rule and to the abbot as the representative of Christ so that in all the observances of the Rule one may come to that perfect love which casts out all fear. St. Bernard had been trained by Stephen Harding at Cîteaux and one may see in this statement the clear integration of the cistercian interpretation of the Rule, expecting the fulfilment of the observances to be the essential means by which the monk comes to know God.

We can separate out three emphases which the cistercians gave to their following the Rule in its purity. They are: solitude of place and silence; simplicity; and the practice of realistic manual work.

Solitude of Place and Silence

Monasticism was born in the deserts and uninhabited places of Egypt, Palestine and Syria in the fourth century. This attempt to live out christian discipleship apart from society in the deep stillness of the desert places brought a man

63

face to face with God in his heart and consequently led him to be also confronted by all that was not of God—evil suggestions, selfish desire and the lure of the things that had been left behind. The support and inspiration of others in this search for God in community life as provided for by the Rule of St. Benedict in the sixth century in no way mitigated the austerity of the inner work of the spirit. The Rule is very explicit about the need for separation from society as a condition for the monk of truly seeking God. 'The workshop in which the monk shall diligently execute the tools of the spiritual craft, is the enclosure of the monastery' (Ch. 4). So it is that as far as possible everything necessary for the life of the community shall be within the enclosure. To be compelled to wander outside the monastery 'is not at all expedient for their souls' (Ch. 66). The monk is to practise silence in this carefully arranged solitude of the community—'Not to love much speaking, but rather to listen gladly to holy reading and to apply oneself frequently to prayer' (Ch. 4).

In the rather romantic account of the arrival of the founders of Cîteaux, the *Little Exordium* tells us that 'This place, situated in the diocese of Chalon, was inhabited only by wild beasts, since it was at that time unusual for men to enter there because of the density of the woods and thorny thickets. Arriving at this place the men of God found it all the more suitable for the religious life which they had already formulated in their minds and for which they had come here, the more despicable and inaccessible they realised it to be for seculars.'[5] The site of the cistercian monastery is a 'desert'—that is, a solitude where Christ is to be found in the company of those who are called to follow Him under the Rule of St. Benedict. There is a sense in which the cistercians were, like Christ, driven into the desert by the Spirit to find reality. It is there they found the means to be obedient to God of which the uninterrupted prayer of the Spirit, filling the heart of the monk, is the fruit. Obedience, according to the Rule, 'becomes those who hold nothing dearer to them than Christ' (Ch. 5). And obedience implies listening attentively to what God is saying. There is no doubt that the cistercian founders wanted the desert solitude in order that their awareness of the Word of God, on whose account they were called to be monks, should be intensified. In the words of the *Institutes*, they came into the solitude of Cîteaux to become 'the new soldiers of Christ, poor with the poor Christ'.[6]

Simplicity

One of the reasons for the spectacular growth of the first monks in the fourth century was that many christians of the time considered that in the acceptance of the christian religion by the state after the peace of Constantine, there had been a fatal compromise with the standards of the world. Many flocked into the Church who perhaps considered the christian religion as the respectable thing to take on. But the renunciation and asceticism of the monks was by no means just a protest against superficial religion. Nor was the flight to the desert the way of escape from an intolerable spirit of compromise as from a contagious disease. The word of Jesus to the rich young man as recorded in Matthew (19. 21), 'If you would be perfect, go, sell all that you have and give to the poor, and you will have treasure in heaven', was taken by St. Antony the Great to be a personal call from the Lord to himself. He believed that this invitation offered

66

to him the means by which he would be led into the fulness of the mystery of Christ. To be 'perfect' was not understood to mean that the monk's vocation is the guarantee of a higher state as a reward for self-sacrifice and ascetic effort but simply what the Greek word (*teleios*) of the New Testament implies—'if you would reach the *goal*'. For all of us, the goal, perfection, is to attain to the stature of the fulness of Christ, and for some of us the means to that is by the radical renunciation of the monk.

The Rule of St. Benedict requires that there should be nothing superfluous in food or clothing and that everything shall be common to all in the monastery, quoting Acts 4. 32, 'let all things be common to all, nor let anyone say that anything is his own' (Ch. 33). Having given everything away on becoming a professed member of the community the monk lives in dependence upon God, relying upon the abbot and community to supply all his needs. It is evident, too, from a careful reading of the Rule that the monastery should be very simply provided for. It is a place where if possible all the necessary things 'such as water, mill, garden and various crafts may be within the enclosure' (Ch. 66), and if it is to be the home of the monk, and the house of God, it can nevertheless be best described as the 'workshop' (Ch. 4) in which the community practises its spiritual craft.

The cistercians wished to return to this simplicity in a variety of ways which broke with the customs of their contemporaries. According to the *Little Exordium*, 'lest anything remain in the house of God—where it was their wish to serve God devoutly day and night—that savoured of pride or superfluity or that would ever corrupt poverty, the safeguard of virtues, which they had chosen of their own free will, they resolved to keep no crosses of gold or silver but only painted wooden ones; no candelabra, but only one of iron; no thuribles, but only of copper or iron; no chasubles, but of fustian or linen, without a pallium of gold or silver . . . They gave up entirely the use of all pallia and copes as well as of dalmatics and tunics . . . Moreover they explicitly ordered that altar cloths be made of plain linen and without ornamentation and that the cruets be without gold and silver.'[7] Although the earliest buildings of Cîteaux have not remained, it is certain that the same austerity was maintained in the architecture

68

of the church and the cloister.   There was no spirit of puritanism in all this, but only the desire to express outwardly their fidelity to their inner spiritual call and the norm of the Rule.   There was good taste and excellent workmanship, inspired not only by Stephen Harding but also by St. Bernard in his conviction that the house of God and the cloister should be so constructed that it should give a foretaste of the luminous harmony of the pattern of the heavenly Jerusalem.   At Fontenay, where the monastery dating from 1130 still stands, Augustine's perfect ratio of squares and cubes is a conspicuous feature of the design; 'each aisle bay is a square in plan and each square is made into a cube inasmuch as the height of the vault is the same as the width of the aisle'.[8]

Nowhere was this desire to maintain an austere simplicity so widely felt as in the celebration of the liturgy in church.   During the previous two centuries numerous psalms, litanies and processions had been added to the Divine Office so that the *opus Dei* became almost the sole work of the monks under Cluny's rule.   The cistercians simply omitted everything the Rule of St. Benedict did not prescribe.   They wholly ignored some current liturgical practices so that during Lent, for example, the cistercians continued with the normal ferial office until Easter without dropping the alleluia. Although much of this revision was of a conservative character, chiefly on account of the paucity of accurate information about liturgical usages in the Church, the simplification enabled the monks to have a much more balanced horarium in which both reading and work, as well as the *opus Dei*, had an essential place.

It is in the matter of food and clothing that the cistercian founders appear to us to be most literal in their appeal to the purity of the Rule. In the *Institutes* they say, '(The abbot and brethren) rejected what was contrary to the Rule, namely full mantles and furs, as well as shirts of fine linen, cowls, and breeches, combs and blankets, mattresses, a wide variety of dishes in the refectory as well as fat and everything else which was against the purity of the Rule'.[9] And yet, this austerity in the use of things serves to show how dedicated the founders of the New Monastery were to their principle that the monastic observance must be an integrated one, following the spirit of the Rule. It was not the 'simple' life for which they were striving but the appropriation for themselves of the death and resurrection of Christ by whom, in their baptism and monastic call, they had been apprehended. It was a determined effort to put into practice the admonition of the Rule which they cherished so much—'Let them prefer nothing whatever to Christ' (Ch. 72).

Manual Work

Integration of one's life implies balance. It was a right instinct that led the founders of Cîteaux to renounce all the endowments and income through tithes and churches and serfs by which the monasticism of the eleventh century was supported. The *Institutes* say, 'Where the blessed Father Benedict teaches that the monk must avoid worldly affairs, there he distinctly explains that these things must not have any place in the actions or in the hearts of monks who must live up to the etymology of their name by fleeing all these things . . . Thus having rejected the riches of this world, the new soldiers of Christ, poor with the poor Christ, began to consult with one another as to the question of the way by which, and with what work or occupation, they should provide in this life for themselves as well as for guests who would come, rich and poor alike, whom according to the Rule they should receive as Christ.'[10]

If the christian life ought always to be earthed in the world but not *of* the world, the life of prayer of monks requires a realistic work which provides both for their upkeep and for the spiritual fitness of their lives. In Chapter 48 of the Rule it is stated that idleness is the enemy of the soul and that 'they are truly monks when they live by the labour of their hands'. The monastic call is not to live in penury or destitution; and poverty, understood as deliberate hardship so as to live in sympathy and compassion with the the deprived, belongs to a different vocation. The monks in the Egyptian desert were industrious in their own way, belonging to a culture which was content with very little in the way of material things. To pray, to read, to weave baskets and to welcome visitors were all essential ingredients of the simple work of God to which they had given their lives. St. Benedict, in a more developed culture, did not envisage that the monks would necessarily be able to do everything for themselves without help; but it was clear to him that this was the ideal. 'If the circumstances of the place or their poverty require them to gather the harvest themselves, let them not be discontented . . . ' (Ch. 48). It is clear from this that the heaviest work was normally done by others.

The cistercians, in order to fulfil their ideal of living from their own land and by the labour of the monastery, found a practical problem in getting all the work done and still maintaining their balanced day of worship and reading. In an agrarian economy vast tracts of land had to be farmed efficiently in order to support a monastic community. The solution to the problem lay in admitting *conversi* or lay-brothers to the community who would do most of the field work. This proved to be a historical decision for it was through this highly organised labour force that the cistercians were able to expand so rapidly throughout Europe. *Conversi* seem to have been admitted to Cîteaux some time in the second decade of the twelfth century when its lands were increasing during the abbacy of Stephen Harding. It was certainly a compromise solution, despite its usefulness. And yet

73

that most pressing of difficulties—the economics of the monastic life—was solved, for the time being.

What place do we visualise this kind of monastic life taking in the Church and in the world today? Cistercians still stand for these intentions of the founders of Cîteaux in which the balanced routine of prayer, reading and manual work is lived continuously, day in and day out, in the solitude of the monastery.

From the outside a cistercian community of men must seem to be a very static, institutional life. That the 'desert' to which they have retired has often blossomed, physically, has been the cause of admiration to not a few people. In the thirteen century a Danish monastery, having no running water, connected a nearby lake with another lake of a higher altitude and produced a fast running canal which has been called one of the greatest engineering achievements of the time. Cistercian horticulture, apart from the extensive and very efficient wool trade and farming in general, employed highly advanced methods which influenced the progress of horticulture in Europe. There was a glass-roofed house at one monastery in 1273 for the purposes of plant experimentation and fruits and rare vegetables were transplanted from France through daughter houses to Germany and eastwards. Today, we in this monastery use a very advanced method of growing vegetables under glass. But the cistercians did not answer the call to become farmers or engineers.

This secluded monastic life is also often compared to a dynamo supplying spiritual power where it is needed. But the whole idea of power implies a busyness which is alien to the monastic way of life. There is a much simpler explanation of the cistercian way of life than either of these two evaluations which look primarily for what the world would call 'results'—it is a journey. Every person born into this world is on a journey to God and the monk is one who enters more deeply into this inevitable journey. It is for this reason that he comes, at the call of Christ, into the desert of the monastery.

The Desert Journey

The cistercian wishes to leave behind him his entire former manner of life. Whether good or bad, one can compare this to leaving the darkness of Egypt where one was in bondage like the Israelites. To go out into the desert was primarily at a call to obey God, to worship him at his holy mountain. The Rule sees this beginning of a monk's life as a setting out on the way of salvation which at first must seem strict and the entrance narrow—it is like setting up a ladder to heaven and we set our feet, not without trepidation, on the bottom rungs.

Entering the monastery, Christ is found in the midst of the community. He is the Rock who will slake our thirst in the desert, for his is the life-giving water. We are expected to voyage with the brethren on the pilgrimage the entire community as a body is making. The destination is the Promised Land which is the fulness of the kingdom of the Father. The paradox about this journey is that already, here and now on our way, we attain to some foretaste of the end, for the victorious Christ enables us to participate in his journey's end in prayer and the sacrament of eucharist and in genuine love for one another as he has loved us.

The monk soon finds that there are many enemies to face on this desert journey. Not only the crossing of the Red Sea where all that we have left behind pursues us, but the enemies of self-will and discouragement in the face of the vicious onslaughts of pride and sloth, envy and malice and all deceitfulness. The man who thinks that the right ordering of material things is sufficient and is happy with a superficial contentment about the goodness of monastic community life is avoiding the real thing. St. Aelred says that, 'He who shirks spiritual warfare in this life is no better than a beast'.

The monastic community is really tested in its voyage. In the nature of things, could it be otherwise? Both the individual monk and the whole community have moments of purifying struggles which are but the hand of God drawing on those who have dedicated themselves especially to a life of love, preferring nothing whatever to Christ.

St. Benedict is the new Moses who is seen at the outset of the journey as the leader of all those who take up the challenge of following Christ in this road of obedience. The trials of the beginning of a monk's life are seen in the light of conforming his life to a law—albeit a law of love. Only gradually, as it were when he reaches a certain point in his monastic

E

journey, does he reach the Jordan and he discovers that his leader is the risen Jesus, the Lord himself who makes always to go further in order to stimulate our desire to enter into deep communion with him by asking him into the heart. 'O taste and see that the Lord is good!' The experience of God is the goal of cistercian life, through the appropriation of the adopted sonship with which Christ has clothed us. Both the active Martha and the contemplative Mary live in each one of us and coexist in the same community—each desiring to serve the Lord alone, work alternating with stillness, each contributing to the needs of the whole body of the brothers as they journey on towards the homeland, the new Jerusalem.

The monastic 'caravan' is only one of the many parts of the Body of Christ journeying through this New Age towards the fulfilment of the Father's purpose for all mankind and for all creation. It is in this cosmic setting that the true dynamism of the cistercian community's corporate response of faith and hope and love to Christ can be recognised. The exterior observances of the Rule and the desire to follow that Rule in its purity, enable the cistercian to take his predestined place in the purpose of God. He is a man who has entered into an integral way of living in Christ in order that he may come to true love—to become the friend of God, and in that relationship with Christ in the community to let his heart be opened by God for all men to share in the living Word.

Aelred Arnesen

Ewell Monastery,
West Malling,
Kent.

Notes

[1] R. W. Southern, *Western Society and the Church in the Middle Ages*, pp. 34-35.

[2] L. J. Lekai, *The Cistercians*, p. 459.

[3] ibid., p. 461.

[4] Letter 142.

[5] Lekai, op. cit., p. 452.

[6] ibid., p. 459.

[7] ibid., pp. 460-461.

[8] ibid., p. 269.

[9] ibid., pp. 458-459.

[10] ibid., p. 459.

Benedictine Insight
for the Divine Office Today

Benedictine spirituality has traditionally placed an enormous emphasis upon the role of the liturgy in christian life. This concern for the liturgy has led in history to significant contributions by benedictine scholars in the study of liturgical sources, and also to the emergence of certain monastic communities as centers for the celebration of the liturgy as a type of apostolate to the whole Church. The summons of the Holy Rule to daily corporate prayer has been the basis in benedictine history for the development of a liturgical piety which has deeply influenced the evolution of patterns of worship in the West. Indeed, the current Liturgical Movement, as it bears fruit in new authorized rites in the various churches, owes much to the groundwork laid in earlier generations by benedictine communities dedicated to the *opus Dei*.[1]

Yet having acknowledged that debt, it is important for us to look at the monastic contribution with an honest and critical eye. We must ask *how* the insights of benedictine liturgical experience may best be appropriated today for the benefit of the prayer life of the Church as a whole. That the benedictine tradition of worship offers such insight can scarcely be questioned; the issue only is how that insight is to aid the wider body of christians in the development of an authentic liturgical piety suited to their own mode of life. History offers us examples of the taking over of monastic liturgical models as a type of blueprint for the liturgy of the parish. The results of this approach have, on the whole, been negative. The fault for this has not been in the models themselves, for these have been generally appropriate to the monastic life-style. The problem has been rather in an approach to liturgy in terms of fixed models.

The parish community is quite different in style from the monastic community, and these vary a great deal even among themselves. It is not possible to apply a liturgical model, as it were, from the outside. An authentic liturgical model develops in accord with the underlying and fundamental structures of each particular type of christian community. The same principle applies to the differences of life-style of the persons who make up these various types of community. The life pattern of a monastic, whether ordained or not, is quite different in character from that of a priest or layman whose vocation is lived in secular society. One of the most disastrous developments in the evolution of the liturgy was the attempt to impose the monastic model of liturgical piety upon christians as a whole. The result was the privatization of the Divine Office among secular clergy, and the virtual loss of the office from the general liturgical experience of the laity.

The insight offered to the Church's prayer life by the benedictine liturgical experience lies along another path. What the benedictine tradition offers is a basic set of liturgical priorities, priorities which possess a wide range of applicability to questions concerning corporate prayer facing us today. Those of us who do not live in monastic communities and whose vocations call us to parochial, or academic, or newly-emerging patterns of christian community, cannot take over the monastic models for our daily round of prayer. But we can look to the monastic tradition for the clarification of priorities in prayer.

When the two-fold pattern of the Divine

Office in the *Book of Common Prayer* was developed by Archbishop Thomas Cranmer, he essentially adapted the monastic pattern to a form which he thought would be appropriate to the clergy and laity who lived in secular society. In many ways, this was one of the most successful adaptations in liturgical history. Liturgical reflection in our own day, however, suggests that Cranmer did not reform the office as appropriately as he might have, that he perpetuated certain monastic models and at the same time failed to restore the special character of the ancient popular forms of common prayer. The underlying intention of this essay is to consider the question of the Divine Office today against the background of the character of the monastic office and Cranmer's reforms. Our contemporary situation requires us to look for insight in this historical material, and an honest recognition of its impact in the past. At the same time we are called today as christians to be persons of prayer who must cut through our history to shape patterns appropriate to our life today.

Historical Background

It is only from the fourth century onward that we have clear evidence for the corporate celebration of a regular daily office.[2] The evidence suggests that these offices did not include readings from Scripture but were made up rather of psalms, hymns and prayers of intercession, and were concerned more with praise and adoration than with any didactic or evangelical emphasis.[3] The use of the psalter in these popular offices was limited to a very few psalms selected for their appropriateness to the time of prayer. There seems to have been little variation in the appointed elements, thus permitting a familiarity which encouraged general participation. Although other times of prayer were kept, often as informal or private occasions of prayer,[4] the two principal times for the gathering of the church were at the beginning and at the close of day.

Tertullian referred to these prayers as *orationes legitimae*, the obligatory or prescribed prayers.[5] They were not a special duty of the clergy but of the local church as a whole. This two-fold pattern of popular prayer was an ordinary part of the liturgical life of the Church. Although it offered the clergy an opportunity for teaching the gathered people,[6] it was essentially an action of praise, brief and ceremonious in style, and shared in by a significant representation of the local church.[7]   Generally known as the 'cathedral office', because this form flourished in the great cathedrals and was often presided over by the bishop assisted by a whole range of other ministers, its simplicity of form differed significantly in character from the monastic office which eventually spread outside the monasteries and usurped its central place as the chief non-eucharistic form of christian prayer.[8]

The character of monastic life led to the development of a concept of the Divine Office quite different from that of the general Church community.   Two significant characteristics may be singled out as monastic in origin: 1) the idea of the recitation of the entire psalter in the course of the office, and 2) the reading of Scripture according to the principle of *lectio continua*, that is, the reading of the various books of the Bible in course.   The impact of these two customs was to create offices of considerable length. The brevity, simplicity, and invariability of the cathedral office found few echoes in the monastic pattern. In due course, the popular pattern lost out as monastic piety came increasingly to be regarded as the ideal. Whereas the origin of the integral recitation of the psalter seems to have been as a basis for meditation, and the reading of long passages of Scripture was incorporated by the monks for didactic purposes, their effect was to produce a verbally overladen pattern of awesome proportions.[9]

It is no surprise that this elaborate pattern of prayer became an impossible burden for the secular clergy. It was thoroughly unsuited to a life of active pastoral ministry. For most it became a painful duty which, to judge from various ecclesiastical legislation of the Middle Ages, was to be gotten around by any means which might be devised. Recitation of the Divine Office in choir virtually disappeared from the life of the typical diocesan priest, although it was expected that the various hours would be said in private. The office had come to be a clerical duty, based upon the monastic model, and recited privately as a matter of personal discipline and devotion. For the majority of christians, the Divine Office had given way entirely to the Mass as the primary liturgical focus of christian piety. This was very much the situation at the time Thomas Cranmer began his adaptation of the office for the English Church.

The Anglican Daily Office

It is possible that Thomas Cranmer's greatest liturgical legacy is to be found in the two-fold office which he produced for the *Book of Common Prayer*. For over four hundred years it has been the only reasonably successful example of a daily office in regular use among the various traditions. Whereas the Roman Church maintained the clericalized character of the medieval office and encouraged a predominantly Mass-centered piety among the laity, the Protestant churches recovered lay participation in non-eucharistic worship by displacing the Mass from its fundamental relation to the celebration of the Lord's Day.

Although Anglicanism also lost for some time the integral association of the Eucharist

90

with every Sunday, it did keep the popular celebration of the office as the daily prayer of the Church. Today, when voices within the various liturgical traditions express anxiety about a tendency to over-eucharistize, Anglicans may rejoice that their heritage offers the riches of this tradition of daily prayer which Louis Bouyer has described as 'a Divine Office which is not a devotion of specialists but a truly public Office of the whole Christian people. ... The Offices of Morning Prayer and of Evensong, as they are performed even today in St. Paul's, Westminster Abbey, York Minster, or Canterbury Cathedral, are not only one of the most impressive, but also one of the purest forms of Christian common prayer to be found anywhere in the world.'[10]

Yet admitting the quality of Cranmer's contribution in this regard, we face today, especially with the recovery of a fuller recognition of the place of the Eucharist in christian piety, a type of crisis in connection with the Divine Office. The pattern which we have inherited from the Prayer Book tradition runs the risk of either failing to serve our authentic needs for non-eucharistic forms of prayer, or else of being completely displaced by the Eucharist as the only expression of corporate piety.[11]

It is ironic that the dominant characteristics of the Prayer Book offices are precisely the two monastic elements which overwhelmed the cathedral office of the early medieval period. In other words, although our offices of Morning and Evening Prayer are intended to be forms for the use of the whole Church and not merely the clergy, they are characterized by a verbosity quite alien to the popular offices upon which they would seem to be modeled. This is perhaps a testimony to the literary quality of Cranmer's work, but it may also alert us to problems before us today.

The fact is that the Daily Offices are far less used by the laity than they seem to have been in the past. They are more generally associated with the clergy, although here, too, the recitation of the offices seems greatly weakened in practice. This is not the place to analyze the reasons contributing to this situation, but given the evidence of a great desire for daily prayer in the lives of countless christians, it would seem that the Anglican forms as traditionally structured do not serve as vehicles for this purpose.

Has the time come when we should at least restore as an option a form of daily office more consciously shaped according to the principles of the cathedral type? The monastic accretions do not serve for us the purposes which they served (and may yet serve) for monastics. The psalms as recited typically in our parishes, as a block of rote verbiage, hardly serve as a basis for meditation. (The use of responsorial psalmody, preferably sung, at least offers an opportunity to reflect upon the text as it is repeated by the cantor.) The use of the psalms in course simply compounds the difficulties by over-riding the diverse character and appropriateness of the various psalms.

Similarly, the didactic character of the scriptural readings seems to be far more appropriate to the Liturgy of the Word of the Eucharist, in which the readings serve as the basis for either the kerygmatic or didactic intentions of the preacher. If the purpose of the readings is for Bible study, then it would seem to be more effectively accomplished in a quite different context.

Benedictine Priorities

We have been moved to reject the two dominant characteristics of the monastic Divine Office as inappropriate, at least on many occasions, to the non-eucharistic prayer of the Church as a whole. The rejection grows not from some basic fault in monastic piety, but rather in the wholesale adoption of that piety and its forms for christians generally. At the beginning of this essay, however, it was suggested that the significance of the benedictine tradition for christian prayer today is not to be found in the imposition of its liturgical forms as models, but rather in the priorities for prayer which that tradition places before the Church.

First, the Holy Rule clearly holds before us the necessity for daily prayer in the lives of christians. By the time of St. Benedict, the fusion between cathedral and monastic office was already taking place, but the evidence suggests that during his time the cathedral type continued to flourish and to be the twice-daily occasions for the Church to gather for prayer. This fact should help guard us against any attempt to program all people to the same patterns of prayer. Communities of christians vary; the lives of individual christians vary; but all of us are called to a vocation of daily prayer by virtue of our membership in the Church. That prayer will take diverse forms because of our diverse human situations, but the priority of daily prayer touches us all.

Second, the Rule of St. Benedict establishes corporate prayer as the normative pattern of christian prayer. As my life is involved with others, and as I share my life in the Church with others who live by the same faith, so my prayer should express that joint participation in God's saving work. Salvation is not individualistic, and neither is prayer. Yet as clear as the Rule is in revealing the corporate character of the Church's prayer, it nevertheless recognizes that there are occasions when the christian finds himself away from his community and even alone. St. Benedict's insistence on monastic stability in community reminds us that the Church as our family, the source of our identity, is always our point of reference. We can have no privatized spiritual world. Even our most solitary acts of prayer find their origin in our participation in the life of the Church.

Finally, the Rule does not absolutize even the models which it offers. After proposing an elaborate scheme for the inclusion of all the psalms within a weekly cycle of prayer, St. Benedict allows that some other scheme might also be used. Although, for monastics, he would have considered anything less than the complete psalter an indication of laxity, the priority which I see here is the principle of flexibility and the secondary nature of all our forms or patterns. In matters concerning corporate prayer, this is an important priority to keep in mind. The liturgy must point beyond itself. Its end is God only. If we sit too tenaciously upon our forms, they run the risk of becoming idols. The monastic priorities are regularity in prayer, the ecclesial nature of prayer, and the need for a willingness to adapt. These are priorities for all christians.

Louis Weil   *Nashotah House,*
Nashotah,
Wisconsin,
U.S.A.

Notes

1 A useful article on the monastic contribution to the liturgy is: *Monks and the Future of Worship*, by Nathan Mitchell, in *Worship* 50 (1976), pp. 2-18.

2 Although it is likely that some ecclesial ordering of the hours of prayer existed from much earlier times, our purposes in this essay are best served by focusing on the clearer evidence available to us from the fourth century.

3 A useful summary of current opinion on this subject is provided by Paul F. Bradshaw in his article *The Origins of the Daily Office*, published in *Alcuin*, 1978.

4 Cf. Hippolytus of Rome, *Apostolic Tradition*, 41.

5 *On Prayer*, 25.

6 Cf. Hippolytus, op. cit., 39.

7 Cf. Eusebius of Caesarea as cited in J. G. Davies (ed.), *A Dictionary of Liturgy and Worship* (1972), p. 326: 'The command to sing psalms in the name of the Lord was obeyed by everyone in every place'.

8 The work of Juan Mateos, S.J., is especially illuminating. Cf. his two articles, *The Origins*

97

of the Divine Office, in *Worship* 41 (1967), pp. 477-485, and *The Morning and Evening Office*, in *Worship* 42 (1968), pp. 31-47.

⁹ Cf. the daily schedule of the monks at Cluny, in Noreen Hunt's *Cluny under Saint Hugh 1049-1109* (1968), pp. 99-123.

¹⁰ *Liturgical Piety* (1955), p. 47.

¹¹ Cf. the article on this question by W. Jardine Grisbrooke: *A Contemporary Liturgical Problem: The Divine Office and Public Worship*, in *Studia Liturgica* 8, pp. 129-168; 9, pp. 3-18, 81-106.

Extended Note

It might give added weight to Fr. Weil's argument if we look at what monastics themselves have done about their office in the liturgical renewal following Vatican II. Permission to experiment was given both to benedictines and cistercians and in the last ten years or more full advantage has been taken of it. It is sufficient perhaps to quote the Ordo of the English Benedictine Congregation: 'There will be no common benedictine breviary in the future'. This brief sentence bears out Fr. Weil's caution against imposing a common pattern of prayer on everyone. Both in the Roman Church since the reforms of Pius V (1568) and in the Church of England with the enforcement of the Prayer Book under Elizabeth I, liturgy became something imposed from above. In reality it should grow out of the community of the local church and become the expression of its corporate life. Guide lines will be needed and for benedictines these have been provided in the *Directorium* for the celebration of the *opus Dei* and in the *Thesaurus Liturgiae Horarum monasticae*, a repository of texts and structures on which any congregation and monastery can draw in revising the office. The following are among the options offered which bear particularly on Fr. Weil's thesis: the psalter may be arranged in a one week, two week or four week cycle; at Lauds and Vespers prayers and intercessions may precede the Lord's Prayer; at Vigils there should be one long Scripture lesson, and in the second nocturn a spiritual non-biblical reading.

What has been the result of this permission to experiment ? There has been no lessening of the priority or the importance of the Divine Office, but the recognition that life in the twentieth century is very different from what it was in the sixth, for monks no less than for priests and lay people. A legalistic obedience to a fixed norm has given place to a desire for a genuinely prayerful office in which quality matters more than quantity and whose celebration is compatible with other demands made on the community. The creative liberty which Benedict was free to exercise in his day has characterised this approach and there has been a fruitful pooling of resources both as regards texts and music and in which we, as Anglicans, have been able to share. The trend towards the vernacular has shown the need for fresh material and particularly new hymns. It has also raised the problem of the chant. Plainsong is the perfect expression of the marriage between words and music and though it can be adapted to some languages more easily than others, the result is never comparable to the original Latin. All this has proved a challenge and though the period of change and experiment has often been uncomfortable few communities would deny that it has been a creative and wholly worth-while experience.

Some monastic houses have opted for a four-fold office similar to that of the new Roman liturgy of the Hours, e.g. a Morning Office combining elements of Vigils and Lauds; a Midday Office which replaces Prime and the Little Hours; Vespers and Compline. Others have kept Vigils and Lauds but have adopted the Midday Office. The vernacular is largely the norm in England though some houses retain Vespers in Latin in order not to break completely with the tradition of Gregorian chant. Advantage has been taken of the alternative cycles for the psalms and most houses now have a two-week cycle for Vigils while others have extended it to Vespers and Lauds. This rearrangement still involves, in most cases, a *psalterium currens* though some houses, including our own, have attempted a more selective grouping, e.g. on Sundays the psalms are chosen for their reference to the Resurrection and on Fridays to the Passion. Some communities are experimenting with the actual recitation of the psalms. At Vigils they may be read by one voice, or divided among two or three, and sometimes used responsorially.

The Scripture readings which had been reduced to a fraction during the centuries are a great improvement on those of the old breviaries. Many benedictine and cistercian houses have adopted the lectionary of the new Roman Office. These in length and content are very similar to the new Anglican lectionary, though not as regards the order in which the books are read. In both the principle of track reading is used for the Old Testament, i.e. certain passages are omitted without impairing the essential argument or narrative of the book. In the selection of the non-biblical lesson there is particular scope for creative freedom : patristic, exegetical, current spiritual writing and poetry all have a place.

Finally many monastic communities are including intercessory prayer in the Office, usually at Lauds and Vespers. Benedict in the Rule gives the *Kyrie eleison* its correct name of *litania* and though it is unlikely that this involved a series of petitions, monks and nuns are now introducing intercessions at this point, often spontaneous and of a topical nature.

So it would seem that monastics themselves are endorsing the insights Fr. Weil has singled out: flexibility in the ordering of the office; quality rather than length; willingness to explore new forms rather than clinging to what has always been; a corporate offering of prayer and worship which while springing out of the community is rooted in that of the whole praying Church of God.

St. Mary's Abbey,
West Malling,
Kent.

Benedictines and Christian Unity

Exactly one hundred years ago, when the fourteenth centenary of the birth of St. Benedict was celebrated, the particular contribution of Pope Leo XIII was to propose the establishment of a central college in Rome where benedictine monks from every country and every congregation could pursue their theological studies. The College of Sant' Anselmo on the Aventine Hill did not become a reality until 1887, since many of the abbots regarded the papal project as one more step towards curial control and the transformation of the spiritual family of the benedictines into a centralized modern order— and they were not reassured by the title of Abbot Primate given to the Abbot of Sant' Anselmo.

A higher standard of education for the regular clergy was not the only motive that activated Leo XIII. In 1893 he gave an audience to the student monks of Sant' Anselmo and confided to them one of his deepest yearnings:

'You know how concerned I am for the reconciliation of the Eastern Churches. Well,

I count on you to help me bring it about. I
have often said to myself: I need Benedictines
for this. The Orientals still have a deep respect for them, because they have remained men
of prayer and of the liturgy, and their origin
goes back so many centuries. Be docile and
the pope will be able to make you his helpers
and send you to reconquer the Orient. This
thought was one of the motives that led me to
erect the College of Sant' Anselmo. Among
all the orders, only the Benedictines do not
arouse suspicion in the Orient. When the
students of Sant' Anselmo are familiar with the
Fathers of the Church and with St. Basil and
St. Chrysostom, they will be able to preach in
turn in Greece, at Athens, at Smyrna, anywhere.
If I speak of Greece . . . I think of the whole
Orient, even the Far East. The heart of the
pope must embrace the whole universe. Monasteries must rise up everywhere to bring back
to the truth those who have strayed. It is from
Sant' Anselmo that I want to see these colonies
leave.'[1]

This important address demands some com-
mentary. That it was not an isolated outburst
is proved by a letter Leo XIII sent to Cardinal

Dusmet in January 1887 in which he stated clearly that the foundation of Sant' Anselmo was 'connected with several of our projects, especially in view of the good of the Eastern Church'. It is confirmed also by the encouragement he gave to a Belgian benedictine, Dom Gérard van Caloen, who dreamed of the foundation of a monastery of the Eastern rite. Van Caloen was in fact at Sant' Anselmo in 1893 but two years earlier he had outlined his vision in the *Revue bénédictine*:

'These monks, formed in advance in the liturgy, the language and the customs of the Greeks, will go toward them as brothers, establish themselves there and lead a purely monastic and liturgical life which the Greeks admire so sincerely. It will not be a question of converting them or of proselytizing . . . They will make the Greeks see that the Roman Church does not in the least dream of taking away from them their rites, customs, and ancient and venerable traditions, since she will go even to the point of authorizing Latin monks to adopt them out of love for their separated brothers.'[2]

We shall have occasion to encounter van Caloen again some decades later: for the moment it is sufficient to record that his ambitious programme struck fear into the hearts of his superiors, who quickly succeeded in finding a new and safer task for him: the reform and renewal of benedictine monasticism in Brazil.

Van Caloen's article of 1891 in the *Revue bénédictine* explicitly renounced a proselytizing approach; it envisaged a long term work of *rapprochement* trying to 'dispel little by little the prejudices which still exist against the Roman Church'. For its time, this attitude was remarkably and daringly *avant-garde*. For with Leo XIII we are not yet dealing with an outlook that can really be called ecumenical; we are dealing with a phenomenon which has been called *Unionism*. It has of course its positive features: Leo XIII worked hard to rescue the Eastern Rite Churches (commonly called Uniat) from the progressive latinization that had been forced upon them; he looked too not just for individual conversions but, to quote again his own words, 'for the reconciliation of the Eastern Churches'. But Unionism, it has been said,[3] is solidly anchored on four pillars. The first is an affirmation of faith in the Catholic, Apostolic and Roman Church as the one Church of Jesus Christ, with the only solution for 'heretics' and 'schismatics' being a return to Peter's barque. The second is a method—or, rather, a hesitation between two methods. One of these is to minimize the christian content of separated communities and to concentrate on the individual conversion of their adherents; the other is to minimize the differences and to exploit the existence of the Uniat Churches, both in order to prove the genuine solicitude of Rome for diversity—or, as we would call it today, pluralism—and to make corporate submission relatively painless and indeed attractive. Thirdly, there is a deliberate selection; for the first method is applied to Western Protestantism, the second is preferred for the Eastern Churches, and a certain hesitation between the two marks the approach to Anglicanism. Fourthly, there is usually a strong strategic and politico-religious motivation, with Vatican diplomacy attempting to strengthen its position in various parts of the world and in various sectors of society. Yet, when the force of this criticism has been admitted, it must still be admitted that Leo XIII's approach implied a genuine broadening of the

Roman Catholic Church's theological, liturgical and spiritual horizon, the admission that to be 'Catholic' and to be 'Latin' were not synonymous and even that the Latin and the Greek traditions were to some extent complementary. Above all it demonstrated the beginning of a certain attempt to understand sympathetically the obstacles to union as they were seen from the other side and to look for factors which at a psychological and at a spiritual level would work for convergence, understanding and *rapprochement* rather than exacerbate existing differences. Leo XIII showed real perception in singling out the benedictines for this work; in 1897 he was able to entrust the Greek College in Rome to the benedictines, and during the First World War Pope Benedict XV entrusted the newly founded Pontifical Oriental Institute to the care of the benedictines also.

Nevertheless the most startling fact about Leo XIII's allocution to the students of Sant' Anselmo in 1893 is that it had to wait for thirty years before it found a response. As Father Louis Bouyer has observed, 'the few young monks admitted to this confidence of the aged pontiff went away bowled over, ready and eager to undertake anything their superiors might ask of them in order to put into effect this desire. But nobody ever demanded anything of them at all. The stone thrown into the deep waters of benedictine silence provoked not even the tiniest ripple.'[4]

The response, when at last it did come, was provided by a most remarkable man, Dom Lambert Beauduin. There is no doubt in my mind that he is clearly the outstanding benedictine of the twentieth century; indeed I would argue further that his name should be included in any short list of those christians of our own generation whose influence on the life of the whole Church has been most profound and far-reaching.

Octave Beauduin was born near Liège in Belgium in 1873 and soon after his ordination to the priesthood in 1897 entered a new and enterprising form of social and pastoral apostolate, the Congrégation des Aumôniers du Travail (Workers' Chaplains). He was never to repudiate the experience, and the sympathies and the insights that he gained through this ministry, but he found himself moving away from social activism to a sense of the directly evangelical, pastoral and spiritual nature of the priestly vocation. His personal pilgrimage led him to resign from the congregation in 1906 and in the same year to enter the relatively new benedictine Abbey of Mont-César in Louvain. He entered wholeheartedly into what the Rule of St. Benedict describes as a 'school of the Lord's service' and so found his whole conception of the life of prayer revolutionized by the liturgically oriented spirituality of a benedictine monastery. What had driven him to the monastery was in part a deep but largely inarticulate dissatisfaction with what seemed to him the superficial quality of his life and activity as a secular priest; in the liturgy he was now to find not only the key to his own personal problem but the key to the renewal of the Church.

It was from Mont-César that Dom Lambert, as he had now become, sounded the trumpet call of liturgical renewal. It is not my task here to describe the Liturgical Movement launched at a great National Congress in 1909 at Malines, at which Beauduin, whose participation had been sought by Cardinal Mercier himself, was to provide a paper which can be described as its foundation charter. It must suffice here to quote the judgement of an eminent German historian of the liturgy: 'In a now famous speech to the convention of Catholics at Malines in the year 1909, this extraordinary man appealed courageously for a renewal of the liturgical life of the Church in a speech which made him the founder of a new and powerful movement.'[5] It must however be said, in view of his later activities, that Beauduin's motivation was at once deeply theological and strongly pastoral: it was based on a vision of the Church as the Body of Christ, on the priority of corporate worship, on the need to restore the liturgy to its true rôle of directly nourishing the minds and souls of christian people, and on a reaction to the excessive individualism of so much of the piety of his day. The liturgy emphasizes the true dignity of human nature and the spirit of brotherhood within the Church; already as a liturgist and with reference to the liturgy he had adopted the motto *ut unum sint*—for to him the liturgy constituted 'a powerful bond of union'. This conviction foreshadows Dom Lambert's later concern for ecumenism, in a sense latent and implicit in the realization that had seized hold of him so powerfully when he became a monk—that new awareness of the mystery of the Church which only a truly liturgical spirituality can awake.

There is no time here to recount Dom Lambert's adventures during the First World War as the close collaborator and confidant of Cardinal Mercier in his resistance to the German occupation, his escape from Belgium and his time in England; though it is certainly worth recording that one of the first Anglicans whom he met at this time was G. K. A. Bell, then chaplain to the Archbishop of Canterbury.[6] The story must be taken up again in 1921 when Beauduin was appointed to a professorial chair at Sant' Anselmo and arrived there, as he himself was to put it, 'totally a stranger to questions of unity'. He was not however a stranger to the ideas of monastic renewal; his criticisms of the formalism and rigidity of the life style of the Belgian benedictines and his desire to be allowed to make an experimental foundation of a new type in the diocese of Liège help to explain the enthusiastic alacrity with which his superiors recommended him for the post at Sant' Anselmo.

During his four years in Rome Dom Lambert was profoundly influenced, first of all by his ecclesiological studies and his exposure to Eastern theology and the Greek fathers, and secondly by a number of important friendships and acquaintanceships. One of the most remarkable was with a Polish count, a giant of a man in every way (for he was seven feet tall and, according to Louis Bouyer, bore a striking resemblance to Michelangelo's Moses), who had become the Metropolitan Andreas Szepticki of Lvov and head of the Ukrainian Catholic Church of the Byzantine rite.[7] This man nourished the unshakeable conviction that his own Church could become the bridge-church for the reconciliation of the Orthodox Churches with Rome—on two conditions. The first was to reverse the trend towards increasing latinization within his own Church and to make it more faithfully and more authentically Eastern; the second was to build upon a monastic revival, and for this purpose he had come to the West to look for some educated and experienced monks who would adopt the Eastern rite and give some spiritual leadership and training to the considerable number of largely uneducated peasants he had attracted to his monastic foundation. The style of this monasticism, almost entirely lay, of the greatest simplicity, with great importance attached to manual work and a belief in the renewal of the Church through an authentic liturgical life, could not but appeal strongly to Beauduin. It was one of Szepticki's clergy, Father Cyril Korolevsky —in reality a Frenchman named Charon—who came across the account of the audience given by Leo XIII to the first students of Sant' Anselmo in an old number of the *Revue bénédictine* and showed it to Dom Lambert, with almost immediate and extremely far-reaching consequences.

A very different personality was the French Jesuit, Michel d'Herbigny—later to become Titular Bishop of Ilium and later still to undergo a mysterious disgrace and to lose his episcopal rank and dignity. In the 1920's however he was in Rome as President of the Pontifical Oriental Institute, editor of *Orientalia Christiana* and consultor of the Sacred Congregation for the Oriental Church. Of greater significance, he had gained the confidence of the new Pope, Pius XI, who was looking to the East, and more particularly to Russia, with eager interest. Not only was this a revival of one of Leo XIII's preoccupations; particular urgency of a political and ecclesiastical-political nature was given to this interest by the evolution of communism in what was now the Soviet Union. Had the chance now come for the Roman Catholic Church to take the initiative and establish a strong religious leadership in Russia now that the Orthodox had lost its privileged position and was in singular disarray? In the attitudes of Pius XI and Father d'Herbigny can be detected all the ambiguities of a Unionism which must on no account be confused with genuine ecumenism. D'Herbigny was later to play a sinister role in the machinations that were to lead to Beauduin's disgrace and exile, but at this stage it was he who was to suggest to the new Pope that Dom Lambert could have an important part to play in his projects for the East.

During his time in Rome Beauduin made a chance encounter, sheltering under the same umbrella in a storm, at the door of the Greek College: it was with a certain Mgr. Angelo Roncalli, who had just been appointed Apostolic

Delegate to Bulgaria. He confided to Beauduin that he needed a secretary who could initiate him in the ways of Eastern christians; Dom Lambert was able to supply this need in the person of a fellow Belgian benedictine, Dom Constantin Bosschaerts. The future Pope John XXIII and the future founder of *Vita et Pax* will both figure again in the story we have to tell.

Although Beauduin was now in Rome, Cardinal Mercier had neither forgotten him nor ceased to rely upon him. It was precisely during these years (between 1921 and 1926) that Mercier was host to the Malines Conversations between Anglican and Roman Catholic theologians. Dom Lambert was not directly involved in these; he did not in fact attend any of the meetings. In October 1924 however the Cardinal took the fateful step of writing to Beauduin and asking him to write a paper for him on the historical significance of the pallium and some of the possible consequences of a corporate return of the Anglican Church to communion with the See of Rome. The result was a famous memorandum, *L'Eglise anglicane unie, non absorbée*,[8] read by the Cardinal at the session of 20th May 1925, without the name of its author being revealed; as one of the Anglican participants, Walter Frere, C.R., Bishop of Truro, wrote some years later, it 'took our breath away'.[9] Very briefly, the memorandum was in part an historical study of the pallium and its significance and of the quasi-patriarchal status of the See of Canterbury before the Reformation; in part a proposal for granting similar rights to the Anglican Church (once united with Rome) to those given to the Oriental Catholic Churches, in order to preserve 'all her internal organization, all her historical traditions and her legitimate autonomy'.

Those who have attacked what they would call the basic unreality of the Malines Conversations have not hesitated to single out this memorandum in order to justify their accusation: what in fact could be more utopian than a detailed examination of the ways and means of granting patriarchal status to the See of Canterbury at a time when neither the successor of St. Gregory nor the successor of St. Augustine really believed that corporate reunion was possible? While the French and Belgian Catholics who took part were bitterly criticized by their co-religionists and particularly resented by most English Roman Catholics, they did not all by any means share the same vision of unity. The veteran among them, the Abbé Fernand Portal, who had been profoundly influenced by his long and intimate friendship with Lord Halifax, had travelled a long way from the Unionism we have already described. He had also greatly influenced Cardinal Mercier and was soon, as we shall see, to leave his mark on the thought and vocation of Dom Lambert. A more classically unionist approach was expressed by Mgr. Pierre Batiffol: 'It is no use thinking of a reconciliation of the Anglican Church: that would be utopian, but we can draw nearer to the Anglo-Catholic movement, encourage and enlighten it, perhaps to help to detach it from the political or modernistic elements in Anglicanism'.[10]

The memorandum was to cause Beauduin a great deal of trouble later, when his authorship was revealed and at a time when he needed new friends rather than new enemies. His rather rash suggestion that the new Roman Catholic dioceses in England, created after 1851, would have to be suppressed was not calculated to endear him to Cardinal Bourne or to English Roman Catholics; while his closing challenge, though much more prophetic and positive, did not help his cause in Rome itself:

'What will Rome think of this plan? It is clear that it suggests a principle of decentralization which is not in accordance with the present tendencies of the Roman Curia, a principle that could find other applications subsequently. Would not this be a boon and a great boon? Yet will Rome share this opinion? Nothing can allow us to foresee what the answer will be.'

Dom Lambert Beauduin had produced a bombshell; unfortunately he was to be the principal victim of its explosion. Yet when on 28th April 1977 Dr. Donald Coggan, Archbishop of Canterbury, entered the Vatican, he was greeted by Pope Paul VI with these words:

'The history of relations between the Catholic Church and the Anglican Communion has been marked by the staunch witness of such men as Charles Brent, Lord Halifax, William Temple and George Bell among the Anglicans; and Abbé Portal, Dom Lambert Beauduin, Cardinal Mercier and Cardinal Bea among the Catholics. The pace of this movement has quickened marvellously in recent years, so that these words of hope, "The Anglican Church united not absorbed" are no longer a mere dream.'[11]

The story of Malines is in one sense an interruption in the story of the foundation of the monastery of Amay; in another sense it is essential to the understanding of Dom Lambert's growing understanding of the universal scope of the quest for christian unity and his refusal to allow his foundation to conceive of its vocation solely in terms of the East, let alone solely in terms of Russia. He maintained throughout his life a strong interest in Anglicanism; he was later to meet Lord Halifax, to get into trouble for signing a letter to the Anglican community at Nashdom 'your brother in St. Benedict', and to resume his friendship with George Bell when he had become Bishop of Chichester. Nor did he stop short at Anglicanism; he was to follow with interest and sympathy the work of *Faith and Order* and of *Life and Work* and to communicate the same breadth of vision to his disciples.

A crucial date both in the personal history of Dom Lambert Beauduin and in the evolution of a specific benedictine contribution to christian unity was the Pontifical Letter of 21st March 1924, *Equidem Verba*, addressed by Pope Pius XI to the Abbot Primate, Dom Fidelis von Stotzingen. It seems clear that the Pontifical Letter was in fact the direct result of a letter to Pius XI from Cardinal Mercier and the draft on which it was based was written by Beauduin himself. It was only at Beauduin's insistence that the Letter was addressed to the Abbot Primate rather than to himself. *Equidem Verba* is so important a document that it is worth reproducing in full.[12]

Dearest Son,

Health and Apostolic Benediction. Truly, as we meditate upon the prayer which Our Lord on the eve of his death addressed to his Father *that all might be one*, what could we desire more keenly than to see all Christians make a truce to their hereditary antagonism and re-establish among themselves that perfect unity of the Catholic Church so as to form from henceforth but one flock and one Shepherd.

This desire we address with very special love to the immense population of Russia.

The political calamities which they are suffering at this moment seem to call them to the maternal embrace of the Church.

But in this apostolate for unity who can take a more important part than Western monks, who by their very industrious activity have always deserved so well of the Church and of civil society? Effectively the monastic order owes its origin to the East; established in the West by St. Benedict (whom the Eastern Churches themselves venerate with the greatest devotion as Patriarch of the monks of the West), it had known a marvellous prosperity well before the unhappy separation of the Churches in the eleventh century. Moreover his Order has preserved most faithfully right up to our own day the traditions of the Fathers, zeal for the sacred liturgy and the fundamental elements of primitive monasticism: so many circumstances which render the sons of St. Benedict singularly apt for the reconciliation of our separated brethren.

Wishing to realize without delay so

salutary a project and to adapt it to the nature of the monastic order, we enjoin you, Dearest Son, to write and invite all the abbots and monks of this Order not only to pray urgently to God for unity but also to undertake specific tasks with a view to its realization. It is desirable that the abbots, after consultation among themselves, should choose one abbey of their congregation, or at least one in each country, in which, with the help of the other abbeys, a very special zeal may be deployed and the necessary resources for this most noble enterprise may be built up. Within these abbeys let a certain number of monks be designated with all possible dispatch to apply themselves to the requisite studies—namely, the language of these peoples, their history, their institutions, their psychology, and above all their theology and liturgy—so as to make themselves better qualified for the work for unity. This training will be obtained more easily if you send to Rome, in as great a number as possible, those of your monks most apt for such studies to follow the lecture courses at the Oriental Institute.

Make every effort likewise by the spoken word and by the pen to create in the West a more intense current of zeal and study relative to the points which separate us from the Orientals.

Finally, Dearest Son, it is our great desire that in these abbeys you will turn your attention with all possible charity to the Russian refugees among us.

Should there be among them any who wish to enlighten themselves as to Catholic doctrine or any who, already united with us, wish to be initiated into the monastic life, let them receive from you that brotherly hospitality which you practise so readily. You will apply all your care to make of them loving sons of Holy Church and, please God, good monks.

For these reasons, Dearest Son, do not delay to press forward to the realization of this new project which opens our heart to hope. For it could thus come to pass, with the help of divine grace, that a monastic congregation of the Slavonic rite could one day be instituted. Its central monastery, which in good time will be founded here, will bring together both Western and Eastern monks within a single family in this city, the centre of the Catholic world. It will become the origin and centre of other monasteries which later on, when the opportunity presents itself, can be founded in Russia.

In the meanwhile, rejoicing in this hope, we implore the timely help of God on your behalf, in anticipation of which and as a sign of our very special benevolence, We accord with all our heart both to you, Dearest Son, and to every one of the superiors and members of your illustrious Order the apostolic benediction.

Given in Rome, at St. Peter's, the 21st March, on the Feast of St. Benedict, in the year 1924, the third of our Pontificate.

PIUS PP. XI

It is not necessary to be a highly skilled textual critic to detect that there are, as it were, two layers to this document: Beauduin's original draft and certain modifications in style and in content added subsequently under the influence of d'Herbigny, such as the somewhat restrictive emphasis on Russia and the unfortunate reference to individual conversions. Dom Lambert's convictions on the latter point were strong and unequivocal. One of the reasons why he could not in the end envisage any close collaboration with Mgr. van Caloen was the fact that the latter, who had now set up a charitable and unionist foundation on the French Riviera, had engaged to serve his school and orphanage for the children of Russian refugees a Bulgarian Catholic priest of the Eastern Rite who had no scruples about proselytizing. This confusion not only earned van Caloen increasing distrust from the Orthodox but a rebuke from the Abbé Portal and a very clear statement from Beauduin himself: 'The Russian emigration is the most dangerous of milieux for our work. With them relief work alone should be undertaken. Our work is not directed to that end; indeed, it excludes it.' He spelled this out even more explicitly later: 'Between works of charity and relief on the one hand and the work for unity properly so called on the other there must exist a partition as strict and watertight as possible. Choose between relief work on behalf of the emigrés and the apostolate for the union of the Churches; but, for pity's sake, not the two together and above all not the one for the sake of the other.'[13]

It cannot be said that *Equidem Verba* met with an enthusiastic response from the benedictines; in particular, the Abbot Primate combined a coolness about the whole project with a deep personal distrust of Dom Lambert.

Nevertheless the papal letter could not be ignored. At the beginning of 1925 the Abbot of Mont-César officially informed Dom Lambert that he was authorized to leave Rome and promised him full support and much latitude in the venture of setting up a new community. Beauduin first made a journey to the Ukraine to visit both an Orthodox monastery and Metropolitan Szepticki's Studites at Uniov and then began the arduous but exciting task of gathering recruits and acquiring a house for his foundation of the Monks of Unity—Les Moines de l'Union. A house was found at Amay-sur-Meuse in the diocese of Liège and the noviciate canonically instituted in October 1926. In July 1928 the monastery achieved formal recognition as a priory *sui juris*, independent of all existing benedictine congregations and subject directly to the Holy See. In 1939 the monastery was transferred to Chevetogne in the Belgian Ardennes, where it remains to this day.

At the outset Beauduin laid down the guiding principles of the monastery in a brochure first published in 1925: *Une Œuvre Monastique pour l'Union des Eglises.* In this foundation charter the essential characteristics of the new experiment—though of course they would undergo certain modifications—already find expression. The founder writes of his hopes of a truly international house and of the need to create two chapels in the monastery, one of the Latin and the other of the Byzantine rite. The monastery is to be a centre of prayer, of hospitality, of study and research; a kind of 'bridge' between East and West, initiating Western christians into the Eastern tradition of liturgy, theology and spirituality, and helping Eastern christians to encounter Western Catholicism in an atmosphere of understanding and sympathy. The aims are long term rather than short term (hence the fatal misunderstanding with d'Herbigny); the creation of a climate of mutual trust and understanding. For the purposes of our present study it is perhaps worth quoting the passage in the brochure which speaks of the particular aptitude of the monastic order for the work of reconciliation between East and West.

'The distant origins of the monastic order, going well behind the schism between East and West, its profoundly traditional and liturgical spirit, are a sure guarantee that it will know how to understand the Oriental and Slavonic soul, so essentially liturgical and traditional also . . . Western monks are no strangers to the East. Monasticism is in effect an institution common to both Churches, prior to their separation and possessing a common patrimony. Moreover Western monasticism traces its own origins back to the East. It is only, as St. Benedict says in his Rule, a modest adaptation to our own regions of the Eastern rules, of the Conferences of the Fathers, of their lives, and also of "the Rule of our Father St. Basil". On this account our monks are already an object of sympathy in the East. But if these Western monks consecrate themselves to a thorough study of the traditions, the rites and the glories of the Eastern Church, and if they derive from this knowledge an enlightened devotion to the interests of the East, this monastic institution will go on to win their confidence. It will become a rallying point where those christians who feel the nostalgia for unity can meet each other; a meeting place where souls and hearts, in the serene atmosphere of liturgical prayer, of fraternal charity and of peace, which the monastery—removed from all passionate con- testation—will create, can draw closer to one another, and where the artisans of the definitive reconciliation yet to come can train themselves for that task.'[14]

Besides the creation of a 'bi-ritual' liturgical life, the encouragement of monastic hospitality and of extended visits by his own monks to the East, Dom Lambert had one other essential tool in mind; the foundation of a scholarly review devoted to ecumenical questions. In this de- termination he was encouraged by the veteran ecumenist whom he was learning to revere as his 'guide et maître' and who in turn looked to him as his heir, the Abbé Portal. It was Portal who gave the review, which still flourish- es, the name *Irénikon*, with a backward glance at the tracts on unity written by Dr. Pusey. It was Portal too who stiffened Dom Lambert's resolve not to confine his vision of unity to the East, let alone to Russia.[15]

In fact however Amay, *Irénikon*, and, above all, Dom Lambert himself were accumulating powerful enemies. *Irénikon* was threatened with suppression three times by the Roman authorities in its first years. The Abbot Primate and the majority of the Belgian abbots were suspicious both of the founder and of his foundation. How could they trust a man who was so critical of the dominant 'Beuronian' spirit and style of benedictine monasticism and of the autocratic and prelatical status conferred upon the abbot in that system ? Dom Lambert was fighting for a declericalization of the monastic order; he wanted to see fully professed monks who were under no obligation to take Holy Orders. He had also written words which to those who were too narrowly benedictine in their loyalty seemed almost treasonable: 'It is desirable also that the members of this new monastic institution should take the name of Moines de l'Union purely and simply, without adding any special appellation; Basilians, Benedictines, Cistercians, etc.   That is the ancient custom, still preserved in the Eastern Churches, and it is all the more important to insist on it since the new monastery cannot remain content with western monastic observances but, because of the very nature of its goal, must draw inspiration in many points from eastern monastic traditions.'[16]

In 1926 Cardinal Mercier, Dom Lambert's most powerful protector, had died; in 1928 came Pius XI's encyclical *Mortalium Animos*, which seemed to pronounce Rome's final and total condemnation of the Ecumenical Movement and apparently caused about five hundred subscriptions to *Irénikon* to be cancelled. Beauduin's enemies now included the powerful triumvirate of Cardinal Bourne, the Abbot Primate and Mgr. d'Herbigny, and in December 1928 he was obliged to resign as Prior of Amay. Worse was to follow, for in 1931, after a shameful caricature of a trial in Rome, he was exiled from Amay and from Belgium and was sent a written instruction signed by Cardinal Pacelli (the future Pius XII) ordering him to withdraw for two years to the remote Abbey of En Calcat in the Tarn.   The monastery and its review managed, not without difficulty, to escape suppression but Dom Lambert was not permitted to return to his foundation at Chevetogne until 1951.

Amay, bereft though it was of its founder, pursued its vocation tenaciously and courageously through the difficult years that followed. It was to exercise a profound influence on two men who were to become in their very different ways the champions of the next phase of Roman Catholic ecumenism. The two Frenchmen both came to Amay in 1932 and met each other there. One was the Abbé Paul Couturier of Lyon, the Apostle of the Week of Prayer for Christian Unity, who in 1933 became an oblate of the monastery, taking the name of Benoît-Irénée. The other was a young dominican, Yves Congar, whose acute theological intelligence was turning at the time with particular interest to the problems of christian unity and who some years later was to publish his pioneer study, *Chrétiens désunis*.

Meanwhile in France Dom Lambert Beauduin was beginning to exercise his own very profound influence. He was to play a leading rôle in the development of the Liturgical Movement there, presiding at the inaugural meeting of the *Centre*

137

de Pastorale Liturgique and writing the leading article for the first number of *La Maison-Dieu*. He was also to work quietly but persistently for christian unity. From 1934 to 1939 he served as chaplain to a community of benedictine sisters, Oblates moniales de Ste Françoise-Romaine, then at Cormeilles-en-Parisis and now at Le Bec-Hellouin. He was to help mould the destiny not only of the sisters but of the monks, not least in the awakening of their ecumenical vocation, with its particular concern for Anglicanism which came to the fore in 1948 when they moved to Bec, with its strong historical links with the English Church.[17]

Dom Lambert's eventual return home was naturally facilitated by the fact that from 1944 to 1952 the Apostolic Nuncio in Paris was his old friend, Mgr. Angelo Roncalli. It was as an old man of seventy-eight that he returned in 1951; he was to die at Chevetogne in January 1960 at the age of eighty-six. He was to have one supreme consolation before his death. In 1957 Roncalli, now Cardinal Patriarch of Venice, told a Unity Conference in Palermo, 'I think that we need to return to the method of Dom Lambert Beauduin.'[18] On hearing the news of

the death of Pius XII, Dom Lambert confided
to his friend, Father Louis Bouyer, 'If they were
to elect Roncalli everything would be saved;
he is capable of convoking a Council and he
would give his blessing to ecumenism.' After
a silence a malicious twinkle came into the old
man's eyes and he added, 'I'm confident we
have our chance. The cardinals for the most
part don't know who they're up against. They
are capable of voting for him.'[19] And indeed
they did precisely that! To his explosion of joy
at the election of John XXIII was added his
enthusiasm at the further news that on 25th
January 1959 Pope John had announced his
intention of convoking an ecumenical Council.
To what extent the Pope had been influenced
indirectly in this decision by the man whom
he referred to at Palermo as 'my old Belgian
friend' and who had long been urging the vital
necessity of such a step, we shall probably
never know. It is certain however that Dom
Lambert was a Forerunner and a Prophet, one
of those who had to suffer at the hands of
ecclesiastical authority because, in spite of his
unswerving love for and loyalty to the Church,
he was audaciously ahead of his time. As Dr.

Coggan, the then Archbishop of Canterbury, wrote to the Prior of Chevetogne on the occasion of the fiftieth anniversary of the foundation of the Monks of Unity, 'Dom Lambert's vision is still an inspiration to all those who seek the unity of the Church for which Christ prayed.'[20]

It is astonishing to realize that before 1959 the great appeal of Pius XI to the Abbot Primate of the benedictines had received practically no response except from Beauduin himself. One exception was the setting up of the foundation *Vita et Pax* within the Olivetan Congregation by Beauduin's friend, Dom Constantin Bosschaerts, in 1926, with houses for both men and women, some of them bi-ritual. Among its better known houses are the convent at Schotenhof near Antwerp and the double priory for monks and nuns at Cockfosters in North London. Though the Abbey of Bec belongs to the Olivetan Congregation or 'White Benedictines' it does not belong to the *Vita et Pax* foundation. In September 1959 however there was an assembly of abbots at Sant' Anselmo for the election of a new Abbot Primate, and, at the suggestion of the Prior of Chevetogne and in view of the coming Council, the letter *Equidem*

Verba was read out to the assembly. As a result it was decided that in each country one abbey should assume particular responsibility for ecumenical work; Chevetogne in Belgium, Niederaltaich in Germany, Ligugé in France, Downside in England, and so on.[21] If this particular provision now seems out of date it is not because of a lack of concern for unity in the houses designated but because an ecumenical dimension has become part of the life of so many more benedictine houses, both of men and of women, in every country in the last two decades.

Only in recent years has it become apparent to what extent the benedictine contribution to christian unity can have a wider appeal than that envisaged by Popes Leo XIII and Pius XI. The appeal to Anglicans is not hard to understand. It is not just that there exist communities of benedictine monks and nuns within the Anglican Communion and that these communities are entering into closer spiritual fellowship with their Roman Catholic counterparts, but, even more, that there is a strong affinity between benedictine spirituality and what is often known as *pietas anglicana*; both are sober, moderate, biblical and liturgical in style. What is more unexpected is the appeal of St. Benedict and his Rule to those solidly anchored in the Reformation tradition. The Protestant Churches in the twentieth century have seen an astonishing revival of the religious life, and in the early history of Taizé the Abbé Paul Couturier, oblate of Amay, played no mean rôle. It is perhaps not inappropriate therefore to end with some words from an address given at Coventry in 1967 by the distinguished Methodist historian, Dr. Gordon Rupp.

'The Protestant Reformation contributed notably to the shaping of Europe and it is generally supposed that this marked a halting of what we might call the Benedictine spirit. Well, perhaps that is so, and yet despite all his dire and drastic criticism of monasticism, Luther's priorities—God and conscience and the communion of saints—were those of St. Benedict. Martin Luther went to the Diet of Worms for the same reason that Benedict went to Subiaco, because his conscience was bound by the word of God; God helping him, there he stood, for he could do no other. And the emblem of the Protestant Reformation is a monk wrestling in prayer and studying his Bible, his unconscious mind teeming with the images and words of the Bible, and above all of the Psalms.'[22]

Roger Greenacre   *Chichester Cathedral,*
                                      Sussex.

Notes

[1] Cf. S. A. Quitslund: *Beauduin: A Prophet Vindicated* (Newman Press, 1973), p. 96.
[2] Cf. Quitslund: op. cit., pp. 95-96.
[3] Cf. Etienne Fouilloux: *Dom Lambert entre l'Unionisme et l'Œcuménisme* in *Unité des Chrétiens* No. 29 (January 1978).
[4] Louis Bouyer: *Dom Lambert Beauduin: un homme d'Eglise* (Casterman, 1964), p. 114.
[5] Theodor Klauser: *A Short History of the Liturgy* (2nd ed., O.U.P., 1979), p. 122.
[6] The introduction was due to Canon R. J. Pilkington of Westminster Cathedral.
[7] Beauduin in fact first met the Metropolitan in Belgium shortly before his appointment to Sant' Anselmo.

[8] The French text is published in *The Conversations at Malines, 1921-1925: Original Documents*, edited by Lord Halifax (Philip Allan, 1930).

[9] Walter Frere: *Recollections of Malines* (Centenary Press, 1935), p. 56.

[10] Cf. H. R. T. Brandreth in *A History of the Ecumenical Movement, 1517-1948* (ed. Rouse & Neill, SPCK, 1967), p. 299.

[11] Cf. *Pilgrim for Unity* (CTS & SPCK, 1977).

[12] My own translation from the French version in *Le Monastère de Chevetogne: Notice historique et Informations* (Chevetogne, 1966), pp. 43-45.

[13] Cf. Etienne Fouilloux's contribution to the symposium *Veilleur avant l'aurore* (Chevetogne, 1978), p. 157.

[14] Cf. *Le Monastère de Chevetogne*, (op. cit.) for extensive extracts from this brochure.

[15] Cf. Régis Ladous in *Veilleur avant l'aurore* (op. cit.), pp. 97-133.

[16] Cf. Fouilloux in *Veilleur avant l'aurore* (op. cit.), p. 147.

[17] The community which is now installed at Bec was founded at Le Mesnil-Saint-Loup in Champagne by Father Emmanuel André, who died in 1903. As early as 1883 he began to take an interest in the Eastern Churches and

between 1885 and 1893 directed a review, *La Revue des Eglises d'Orient*, which, although it was largely concerned with the Melkite and other Uniat Churches, endeavoured to help Catholics of the Latin Rite to respect the authenticity and integrity of the Eastern Rite and to appreciate the problems of the Orthodox world. This is one of the factors which have contributed to the ecumenical vocation of the Bec Community.

[18] Cf. Ruth Slade: *Dom Lambert Beauduin* in *Eastern Churches Quarterly* (Vol. xiv, No. 4, 1961), p. 224.

[19] Cf. Bouyer, *Dom Lambert Beauduin* (op. cit.), p. 181.

[20] Prefaced to the volume *Veilleur avant l'aurore*.

[21] Cf. Cuthbert McCann: *The Black Monks and Work for Christian Unity* in *Faith and Unity* (Vol. viii, No. 1, January 1964), pp. 15-16.

[22] *Benedict, Patron of Europe* in *Just Men* (Epworth, 1977), p. 10.

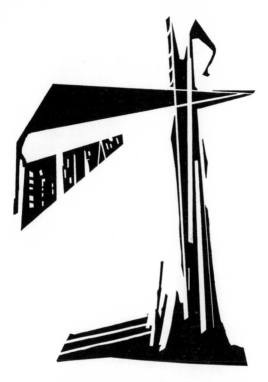

The Benedictine Tradition
and the Family

The family, like the monastic community, is a place where God's love is made incarnate. Each family is its own *ecclesia*, a domestic church, with its series of relationships, with each other, with the local neighbourhood, with God. You start in the place where you find yourself, and with the people who surround you, and they are not necessarily—at any rate after that initial commitment to either the marriage partner or to the community—the people of your own choosing. It is not always easy to accept with gratitude either your fellow members in the community, or the brothers, sisters and parents whom God has given. Working out a series of relationships which can be creative for oneself and for them and lead finally to God, is basic for us all. It is an undertaking which none of us can evade. But even if ultimately we have all to find our own way, there is much in both past wisdom and in contemporary experience to provide guidelines and encouragement. The modern family, struggling to work out its christian vocation within a competitive and materialistic set of values in a world where commitment has become increasingly difficult,[1] may be discovering certain harsh realities which will be of value to those living in community. And in return the Rule of St. Benedict, so firmly rooted in practical and unidealised knowledge of human nature, can form as much for the average christian family as for the monastic family 'a school of the Lord's service'.

The triple link of the monastic vow, stability, *conversatio morum*,[2] obedience, forms the underlying reality of his or her monastic commitment for every benedictine. Still today the vow touches the basic roots of our nature as totally as it has done for the past millenium and a half. To take it seriously and to make it an essential part of any christian life is to come face to face with a means at once of deepening our understanding of ourselves, of others and above all of ourselves in relation to God.

The benedictine vow of stability is not the product of some abstract idealism. Rather it reflects a basic reality, the fact that you must learn to live with and to appreciate your fellow brethren, those to whom (just as in a marriage)

you are committed.   How can we love God
unless we first love our fellow men? Stability of
life-long attachment to one place; commitment
to a life-long marriage; the right balance so
that the parts make up a stable whole—it might
at first seem that these ideals are more in tune
with an earlier Christendom which knew about
hierarchy in the universe and in society, than
with a post-industrial revolution world in
which competitive individualism has come to
play so large a part.   And yet we find that the
benedictine tradition springs from a recognition
of a very deep and fundamental need of the
individual, as vital today as at any time in the
past.   The stability of the relationships with
those around us is also a reflection of the right
ordering and right balance of the elements
within ourselves.   Only thus can true stability
be achieved.   We are clearly told to make sure
that our life is to combine, in due proportion,
the three elements of prayer, study and work.
The *opus Dei*, the heart of it all, is to be fed
and nourished by the intellect and both are
to be anchored in the practical tasks which
mean that the body as well as the mind and the
spirit is brought into play.   The emphasis that

all three are equally important and to be treated with respect is altogether typical of this realistic approach to man. We are to recognise the conflicting elements and the differing needs in our make-up and we are to accept and use them, not deny them. To take the intellect seriously has been a great part of our Anglican heritage and the tradition of learning amongst the clergy is an honourable one. But still there remains a very real danger of failing to maintain this, and to feed the intelligence, particularly where matters of faith are concerned. All too often for the average lay christian the intellectual level of religious understanding remains pathetically out of step with the level expected or demanded in career, or even in leisure pursuits. Yet how can the spirit grow unless it is fed by the mind? But on the other hand how can we guard against becoming so over-intellectualised that we come to think that all knowledge and understanding comes by words, whether spoken or printed? Here work, above all in the labour of the hands, supplies the corrective and restores the balance.

For manual work is something which the twentieth century needs and must increasingly consider seriously. By touching, feeling, by doing the household chores, by handling bread and wood, by opening a tin, we build a small barrier against the torrent of words which seems to dominate and to threaten us and we remind ourselves of the reality of created matter. Manual work can do much for us: it can help us to know ourselves, and it can help us to reach out to others, as well as its most fundamental rôle as a constant reminder of the reality of the Incarnation. 'Work is love made visible' as Kahlil Gibran puts it in *The Prophet*. The connection of work and demonstrating our love for other people is clear. Perhaps we do not always sufficiently allow for it the rôle that Joseph Conrad recognised when he wrote in *The Heart of Darkness* 'I like what is in the work—the chance to find yourself. Your own reality—for yourself, and not for others— what no other man can ever know.'

If the proportion is lost between these three (and for many of us in a sophisticated, articulate society manual labour scarcely exists in any meaningful way any longer) then the sense of right balance within the individual goes, and instead of being mutually creative and healing the parts can become distorted and destructive. Fragmented and broken people are all too common. Harmony, balance, proportion are perhaps even more necessary for us today than they were in the Middle Ages when the Pauline analogy of the whole and the parts was spelt out for all to see in the ordering of society or in the building of great Gothic churches. To accept the differing elements within ourselves may help us towards accepting the differing members of our own society, without labelling and without judging—not always so easy in a country still riddled with class attitudes. But only then can we discover any true sense of being together members of the Body of Christ, inter-connected, inter-dependent, co-inherent. Here is a vision of wholeness which is needed more than ever before in an urban and industrialised world which breeds alienation and isolation.

The vow of stability is the foundation: it underlies both chastity and poverty. If we are to be fully human we need to love and to be loved. We cannot fully know ourselves unless we also let ourselves be known. As we grow into the christian life this giving and receiving of love and of awareness of one another requires of each of us a balance which the ideal of chastity helps us to recognise and achieve. Central is our understanding of God's unique love for each of us and how the experience of love in our own lives mirrors that divine love. And yet it is only too easy for us not to respect each other as creatures made in the image of God. It is all too simple to devalue family and friends by using them to our own advantage. Chastity in its narrower sense involves a sexual restraint, a respect for another's integrity and a refusal to use another as an instrument for our pleasure or self-fulfilment. To accept everyone as he or she is, a person made in the image of God, imposes a similar restraint upon us, in as much as we do not batter them with our demands, or dent them by imposing our views of them, or bend them so as to manipulate them into acting in a way that will please us. Only then will it be possible for each of us to be and to become completely ourselves, and so to grow together to the full dignity and stature of men and women made in the image of God.

In the benedictine tradition there is no vow

of poverty as such. But it is at once clear that it is impossible to fulfil the requirements of the Rule without living in the spirit of poverty. It would be foolish to deny that it is not easy to bring into ordinary family life any sort of meaningful poverty which is more than a gesture to calm our troubled consciences in the face of so much destruction and degradation in the world. But for us in the West poverty is not to be confused with penury. St. Benedict envisaged for his monks material conditions which approximated 'not to the rigours of the Egyptian hermits but to the poverty of the Italian peasant of the day'.[3] The key lies more in our attitude. Most families are not in a position to give much away. But what we have can be seen to be held in stewardship, in trust for others, and particularly in trust for those less fortunate than us. Christ's life on earth was one of self-giving and sharing, however costly. This then is the example: not wanting to possess and to manipulate the people and the things in our lives, but rather accepting them as signs of God's love for us and constantly reminding ourselves of our stewardship, so that we enjoy them in trust, with reverence and with a detachment that means we are not in bondage to them. 'Poverty takes pleasure in a thing because it is, and not because it can be possessed.'[4] Detachment need not preclude enjoyment, for without that there might be a danger of forgetting to give continual thanks and praise for all God's generosity in the good things of daily life. And detachment can still be combined with a sense of worship and awe and respect for these material things of our life. The balance of the two leads to a contemplative stance towards the world.

To take seriously *conversatio morum* brings us into the area of movement, growth, development, an essential counter-point to the vow of stability. This comes out nowhere better than in the amazingly rich and complex ending to the Prologue, where the words that run like jewels catching the eye (and the imagination) are way, entrance, progress, run, persevering, and finally kingdom.[5] Change is one of the hard facts of life that any family encounters and must come to terms with. A new job, uprooting the home, changing schools, a different place to live, are the external changes which often enough complicate the sufficiently demanding changes of personal growth from infancy to puberty, adolescence to middle-age, menopause to old age, and increasingly in the twentieth century as life is prolonged, to senile dementia. What has St. Benedict here to say to ease that path? The answer is that the Rule is a vivid reminder that the christian life is 'not a mere contract here and now, it implies a constantly renewed process, and an inner openness to the future'.[6]

Travel and journeying and personal growth have today become so much part of contemporary thinking, christian and non-christian, that there is a peculiar receptivity towards such ideas, particularly amongst the young. But to travel may be a form of running away, and the growth therapy movement can all too easily become a self-indulgence. Here instead are these ideas incorporated in a framework of christian living which is at once strong and flexible. We are told that 'we must establish a school of the Lord's service' with all that that implies for the continual questioning and growing that is at the heart of schooling at its best. *Conversatio* is a dynamic matter; it means

158

continual conversion; it means time and again reshaping that path which will in the end make us 'Partakers in the Kingdom'. This process, for the individual as for the family or the community, is neither smooth nor continuous. Many of the tensions in family life arise from our failure to face up to the painful and challenging demands of growing and changing. Each successive stage is in some ways *conversatio*, the working out of the full implications of all that is involved in the new step, the new direction, the new dimension.

'Prompt, cheerful, unquestioning obedience' ran the text of Louisa M. Alcott's nursery and doubtless of many other Victorian homes. It is an ideal easily caricatured, and deservedly so, for it diminished the fullness of the individual in the interests of authoritarian paternal power. But the obedience that God wants is not a blind or mechanical conformity which asks nothing from us, and which encourages a way of moronic safety. Rather we are asked for an obedience which makes demands on our intelligence, our sensitivity, and above all, our love. In God's service we shall find perfect freedom. This is the paradox: obedient service and genuine freedom belong together. If we conform our intention to the will of God we are set free from the limitations of our own self-will. This is the mystery. If that obedience does not spring out of fear but out of love and from the heart then it becomes the expression of what we most truly and deeply desire. At the root of obedience is a free, personal, humble, loving surrender to the will of God, a bending of our whole person to the infinite will of God. Thus we discover that through inward assent rather than by outward observance we have established for ourselves the position of becoming collaborators with God. We are brought face to face with the chance to grow in freedom to the full stature of the sons of God.

In the end we want our sons to be free! Family life can be destructive, narrowing, crippling, serving the ends of bolstering up some false expectation or encouraging some false dependency. It is not always easy to learn to be free, and to watch another grow into freedom. But freedom is not the same as anarchy. So the framework and the ordered structure is as vital to the family as it is to the right ordering of any community. The daily, weekly, yearly rituals of life are based on man's need for certainty and security. Small children almost instinctively demand rituals to reassure them. In the years which follow childhood the possibility of enlarging those rituals to encompass the new demands of an enlarging world are almost infinite. Celebration must play a vital part, for as Jean Vanier so rightly points out 'celebration is linked to both family and religious tradition. As soon as it gets away from this it tends to become artificial, and people start to need stimulants like alcohol to get it moving. Then it is no longer a celebration. It may be a party . . . '[7]

The celebration of the Eucharist is the central act of the monastic life; eating together is the main thing that brings the family together. Here we touch the heart of the matter: at once entirely prosaic and yet at the same time utterly mysterious; at once entirely personal and yet also completely corporate. The family sitting round the supper table have, if they so wish, the power to break bread and to share it among themselves in such a way that it breaks down the narrow bounds of individualism and creates a sense of fellowship. 'Meals are daily celebrations where we meet each other around the same table to be nourished and share in joy. They are a particular delight for the body and the senses. So we shouldn't bolt our food under the pretext of having more important or more spiritual things to do than sit at table.'[8] For the very act of breaking bread is in itself symbolic and significant. It is not something that can be done with words; it demands action. But that action can be painful, costly, risky. It is often safer to keep the loaf intact, and not to share our food, our possessions, ourselves. And yet the christian way asks of us precisely this: that we do break and share our daily bread (and that means as well all of ourselves) with each other—whether those others are our God-given family or our God-given community. On that last evening the sharing of the broken loaf and the drinking of the wine were an expression of the disciples' union with Christ and with one another in Him. The broken loaf has become an assurance of our wholeness in Him, and through Him in one another. Wholeness is here, and yet the paradox remains —that that wholeness comes only with breaking and giving, not with hoarding and preserving!

'Let all guests that happen to come be received as Christ for He will say "I was a stranger and you took me in".' For St. Benedict it was central that we should see Christ in other people and that they should find Christ in us. So that to welcome people into our family life and to be prepared to share with them both food and fellowship was very much part of his sense of the right ordering of daily life. Such hospitality means putting aside the lavish and the pretentious entertaining which can become a barrier and prevent others knowing us as we really are. In some families a custom has grown up of spending a moment or two at the beginning of the main meal of the day in thanksgiving and intercession, perhaps making the source of the food on the table, or the presence of a guest, or some particular happening, the starting point of prayers that relate to the immediate occasion. In some families it has also become the tradition to hold hands for this prayer, an act which not only binds the immediate family symbolically to one another, but makes any guest feel that hospitality carries with it a loving acceptance into the family.

But hospitality, and particularly the best christian hospitality of this kind, carries with it a real threat. Keeping 'open house' can become something dangerous, even destructive. Who has not seen vicarages where the door is never shut and where the children suffer, deprived of parental time and concern. Sometimes it has become almost easier to be surrounded by eager students or grateful parishioners or good christian friends making *their* demands than to welcome (in the true sense of opening our hearts to, and being vulnerable to) husband or wife or children. Yet the family must have a still centre, an enclosure, a sacred space if it is to nourish itself. And here the monastic life shows the importance of striking a right balance between enclosure and hospitality. Without it there is the real possibility that those who come will find a hollow welcome, that there is nothing there for it has all been drained away; that the marriage has nothing to give; that the family has nothing to say.

It is all too easy to idealise both marriage and the monastic community as institutions which can be the panacea for so many of the ills of contemporary society. People hoping

to escape the overwhelming isolation and loneliness which is so near the surface today—for
what discussion on social problems does not
emphasise the sense of alienation which is so
widespread—believe that either marriage or
some form of common life provide the answer.
While this may be true it is by no means
automatically so. Both the marriage bond and
the monastic vows involve commitment to
years of difficult, often painful learning. Here
the monastic life shows its wisdom in allowing
the taking of final vows only after a time of
lengthy and serious preparation. In contrast
it has become all too easy to slip into marriage,
even the sacrament of christian marriage, with
thoroughly inadequate preparation. It has become part of our instant world which looks
for instant solutions to its problems. Yet when
seriously, humbly undertaken, both celibacy
and marriage have much in common. Both
can help us to flee from what Jean Vanier has
called 'the wound of loneliness'. 'Those who
enter marriage believing that it will slake
their thirst for communion and heal their
wound will not find happiness. In the same
way, those who enter community hoping that

it will totally fulfil and heal them, will be disappointed.'[9]   Only when we stop running away or using others as a refuge shall we come to fully know ourselves.   'The two vows of marriage and of celibacy which seem so divergent, proceed to link themselves at the depths of our human experience.   Arrived at this degree of intimacy, friends have the feeling of being emptied of themselves, open to the other, and of living in one another.'[10]

'This rule is not meant to be a burden for you.   It should help you to discover and experience how great is the freedom to which you are called.'[11]   The hope of the monastic community, as of the family, is that here we should find the structure and the space to enable us all to become both adult and free. This is after all the promise of the gospel, that we shall grow into the glorious liberty of the sons of God.   And if it sometimes seems that the institutional church prefers enslaving people and putting them into a situation of dependency we must go back to the sources for our spirituality and remind ourselves of St. Benedict's incomparable understanding of human nature.   Because it is so firmly rooted

166

in the acceptance of man as he is, here and now, in this moment and in this place, the Rule asks for no spectacular performances or amazing feats of endurance. It does however assume commitment, possibly the hardest lesson of all for us today. For the prize of freedom is never gained by running away: rather it is the reward of a continuing commitment, a never-ending *conversatio* in the setting of the time, the place and the people whom God has given us.

Esther de Waal   *Canterbury,*
                                              Kent.

Notes

[1] See Dominic Milroy, 'Celibacy: A Monastic Attitude', *Ampleforth Journal*, 1975 (Vol. LXXX Part I), p. 21ff.

[2] *Conversatio morum* is now accepted as the correct reading in RB, though *conversio morum* was very soon substituted for it. *Conversatio* has many meanings: one is a way of life. It

implies a process, whereas *conversio* is only a beginning. *Conversatio* is a difficult word to translate and in effect conversion has to serve for both words.

3 D. Knowles, *The Monastic Order in England*, 1950, p. 10.
4 H. Williams, *Poverty, Chastity and Obedience*, 1975, p. 40.
5 See Daniel Rees and others, *Consider Your Call, A Theology of Monastic Life Today*, 1978, pp. 144-5.
6 Milroy, op. cit., p. 29.
7 *Community and Growth*, 1979, p. 236.
8 Vanier, ibid., p. 238.
9 Op. cit., p. 247.
10 Yves Raguin, S.J., 'Célibat Pour Notre Temps', *Supplément à Vie Chrétienne*, Nov. 1972, No. 151, p. 41.
11 *Rule for a New Brother*, 1978 ed., p. 57.